KIT WILLIAMS

MASQUERADE

Within the pages of this book there is a story told
Of love, adventures, fortunes lost, and a jewel of solid gold.
To solve the hidden riddle, you must use your eyes,
And find the hare in every picture that may point you to the prize.

SCHOCKEN BOOKS · NEW YORK

O nce upon a perfect night, unclouded and still, there came the face of a pale and beautiful lady. The tresses of her hair reached out to make the constellations, and the dewy vapours of her gown fell soft upon the land.

Each picture in this book has a hare in it somewhere. Can you find him in this picture?

AS OLD AS EARTH

ONE OF SIX TO EIGHT

This lady, whom all mortals call the Moon, danced a merry dance in the pathless sky, for she had fallen in love, and the object of her devotion was the Sun.

Although all happiness was in her dance, there was also a little sadness, for whenever the dance led her into the same part of the sky as the Sun, she seemed to simply fade away, and feared the Sun might never notice her.

The Sun, for his part, and contrary to his appearance, was always sad. The one thing he wished for most was a friend. But when people looked at him they immediately screwed up their faces and turned away, which made the Sun think that he must be terribly ugly.

On this night the lady of the pale complexion resolved to make herself known to the Sun by sending him a token of her affection.

To this end she asked the man that plays the music to stop playing for a while; then she plucked from the sea of clouds a most brilliant rose-coloured moonstone. Next, with a little gold taken from the dawn sky, she cunningly wrought a splendrous jewel that was the perfect mirror of her love. It had about it a beauty more permanent than the soft lip or flashing eye, a beauty that is for ever and mocks Time.

When the work was done and the stone was set, the pale and beautiful lady sent for her special messengers, the frog and the hare; the hare because he was as swift as the wind, and the frog for his wisdom, as old as the hills.

"Jack Hare," said she, "listen well. I entrust you with this amulet, and you have but one day to deliver it to my Lord the Sun. Take care, for the way of the little messenger is full of dangers, and yours especially so. Through earth and air and fire and water you must journey, until you reach my Lord the Sun. When you have reached him, show him the jewel and say to him it will be his if he will only give me the answer to this riddle:

> "Fifty is my first,
> Nothing is my second,
> Five just makes my third,
> My fourth a vowel is reckoned,
>
> "Now to find my name,
> Fit my parts together,
> I die if I get cold,
> But never fear cold weather.

"Now be off, Jack, and be quick! And you, frog, you must follow Jack's fortune and help him when you can. Although his legs, like yours, are long, his brain is very small and he may falter in this errand."

AND THE SLEEPY

HOURS OF NIGHT

THE DAY BEGINS

ARE OVER

Jack set off with a great bound and a purposeful expression, pretending he knew exactly where to go and how to get there. But it wasn't long before he was most terribly lost and just jogged along muttering to himself,

"Jack, Jack do this, do that, it's always old Jack Hare, on the go from dusk to dawn, the Hare-bell's always ringing. Jack be quick and Jack in a box and Jack be in the cellar. Well … Jack's as good as his mistress and Ja——— … "

BUMP!

He was so caught up in his own little troubles that he hadn't noticed the Penny-Pockets Lady on the road, selling her fortunes.

"Where's your penny, Long Ears? A penny for your fortune."

"I've no penny," said Jack.

"No penny? No penny? Then why go bumping into people? Have you no manners?"

"No—er—yes, I mean—I just want to know which way to the Sun—er—please."

"If you've no penny then you must answer this riddle:

> "I have a little house,
> Its windows number plenty,
> It's full of flowers that no man picked,
> And you may have it when it's empty."

Jack answered directly, as it was so simple, and licked his lips and whiskers. "Now, which way to the Sun?"

The lady took her hand from her pocket and pointed UP.

J ack looked up and was astonished to see far above him a tiny figure moving from cloud to cloud. Just then, the being swooped down to hover a few inches above his head.

"Good morning, how did you do?" said Jack, remembering his manners but forgetting his grammar.

"Hello, my name's Tara. Tara Tree-tops. Tara's from the Latin you know, and this is my friend Craw. Isn't he handsome?"

"'Ansome, 'ansome, 'ansome," shrieked Craw, and puffed himself out to show off all his pretty feathers.

Nasty bird, thought Jack, but didn't say so.

"We were looking for lost dreams," said Tara, "they're all there up in the clouds, and when the clouds become too full they fall down again; the nasty ones as hailstorms with thunder, and the nice as gentle rain with rainbows. Most of them are quite boring though, like bishops' dreams of corduroy trousers, and bicycles for prime ministers. But sometimes I'm lucky enough to find the feasts of shipwrecked sailors or the palaces of chambermaids ... What's your dream?"

"I want to find the Sun," said Jack.

"Very well," said Tara, "but first you must hear my riddle:

> "I have a little sister
> And in the fields she's seen,
> Dressed in yellow petticoats,
> And a gown of green.
> She's not a bird and cannot sing,
> But she can fly without a wing.

"Now, jump with me and you may find the Sun behind a cloud."

The little hare jumped for all his worth, and up and up he went, over the tree tops, over the church steeple, and over the clouds—but the higher he got, the smaller the Sun became.

NOT AS HIGH

THE SEA SO DEEP

THE HILLS ARE

AS A DREAM

As the hare got close to where the Sun *ought* to be, he heard the most terrible hullabaloo. All the people of earth had taken kettles and pans and sticks and pots, and drums and guns and gongs, and were making a fearful din; and this is the reason why.

The Lady Moon, disregarding all advice given to her by the other celestial bodies, had disobeyed Newton's Universal Law of Gravitation, and instead of continuing her dance in her prescribed orbit, had stayed behind to watch with anticipation the progress of the little hare. It was in thus doing that the unhappy Moon was the instrument of her own undoing. To understand completely, you need to solve this simple riddle:

> I am the beginning of eternity,
> Followed by half a circle, close on by half a square,
> Through my fourth my fifth is seen,
> To be the first in every pair.
> My sixth begins my seventh,
> The end of time and space,
> Now put my parts together to see what's taken place.

When the lady realised what she had done, and saw the hare falling out of the sky and all the other animals running in terror for their lives, she opened her mouth and SCREAMED. A horrible, silent, ghostly scream. The sort of scream that will turn the milk, sour the cream, blight a crop, and lame a horse as it stands in its stall.

All the horrors of the night came forth in this one dreadful scream.

I FOLLOW YOU ROUND AND ROUND AND ROUND YOU FOLLOW ME

The Sun was gone now and the fingers of shadowy night chilled the air. The shrieking and wailing of the people and the banging of their drums reached a climax. Cold panic gripped the animals, and those that only moments before were the deadliest of enemies ran side by side. The fox and the goose, the owl and the shrew, the cat and the hound ran round and round and round until they turned into one huge zoological pudding!

Even the animals themselves were unable to distinguish one from another … In fact, that's how the animals got their tails, but that's in another story. (See if you can count the animals in the picture opposite and give them all names. The answer is at the bottom of the page.)

Jack's small brain was ill-equipped to deal with such a commotion and it was as much as he could do to remember who he was. To save him from losing his wits entirely, he repeated to himself this, his own little riddle:

> "A hopper of ditches,
> A cropper of corn,
> A little brown deer,
> With leathery horn."

This went on until, little by little, the Sun returned and the people, realising that the demon of the night hadn't eaten their Sun after all, stopped the banging and shouting and went back to work.

After carefully disentangling himself from all the other animals, Jack ran off to hide in a tree, just in case it should all happen again.

There are twelve animals: a cat, a corse, a horse, a hog (saddle-back of course), a dog, a dow, a cow, a care, a hare, a ham, a ram and a rat.

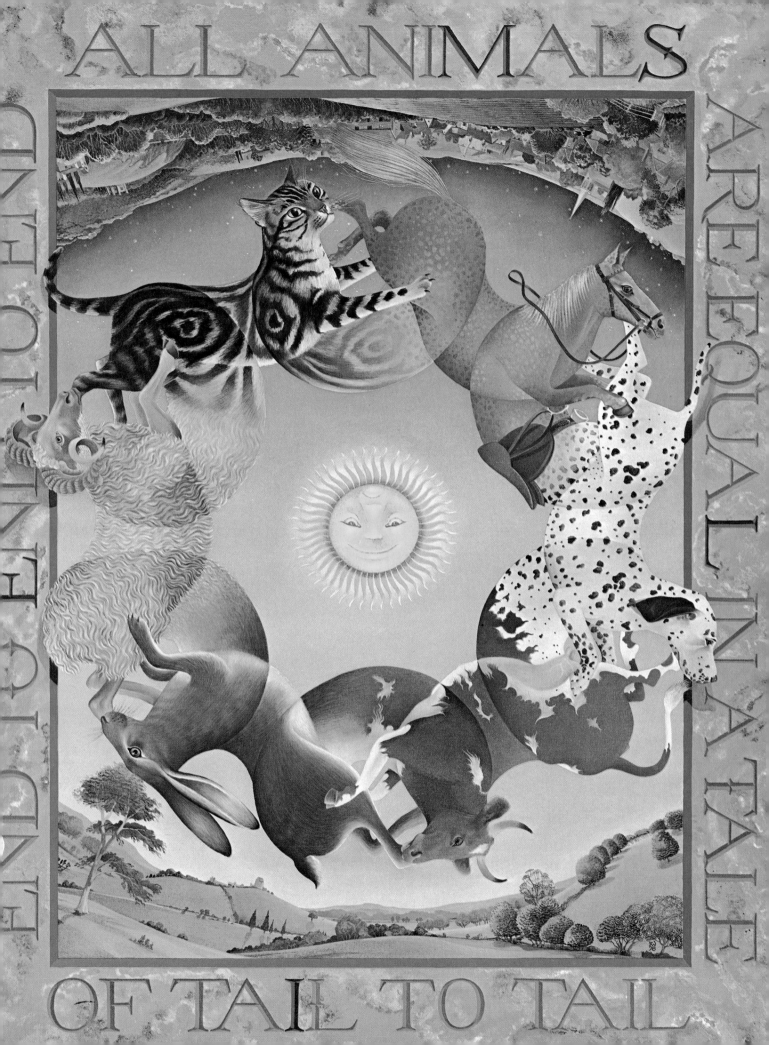

Now that the eclipse had passed, Jack decided to continue his journey, but just then he heard the strains of a sad and sorrowful tune. Looking out of the tree in which he was hiding, he saw a curious little man sitting upon a hillock, playing a violin. Jack jumped down; the little man was the oldest, most crinkled creature he had ever seen, except for an aged tortoise in Dudley Zoo.

"Good day," said the musician. "I am the man that plays the music that makes the world go round. Can I help you?"

Jack related his story and the man stopped the music. "In my opinion," said he, "you require the assistance of the Practical Man. I am but a poet and a musician. You must go to the town and seek him out. To help you on your way, I shall play the Song of the Sun. The Sun is the eye of day, and as long as I play this tune, the day's eye cannot close again."

The man played the Song of the Sun so sweetly that it made the happy daisies grow, and with the sound of the song in his ears, Jack set off. But when he got to the town, all the shops were closed on account of it being Wednesday and half-day closing. However, there was one dingy little antique shop that stayed open, "so as to catch the passing trade". Jack peered in through the window.

"Step in," said the proprietor through the glass, "I have many treasures of antiquity that will take your fancy, or maybe I can show you an hare-loom or two?"

Oh dear, thought Jack, a humorist.

A ROSE IN MAY

RIDDLE DE DUM

A DAISY DAY

RIDDLE DE DE DE

Jack entered the shop.

"Excuse me, sir, are you the Practical Man?"

"Practical! On Wednesday afternoons I could be practically anything. What's up?"

Jack told of his adventures—about the jump, the Sun going out, and the little tortoise-like man. To listen better, the Practical Man took off his glasses and polished them with a red and white spotted handkerchief, but when it came to the bit about GOLD, he popped them on his nose.

"Right!" said he. "I have the solution. Fetch that eye-glass from the window whilst I collect the few other things we'll need."

Moments later, the Practical Man had collected everything in an old cane-back chair. Picking the whole lot up, he waddled out of the shop.

"Come, let us take a little stroll, then some tea, and maybe a little something … to eat."

Jack followed and they went down the street, along the promenade, and down to the beach. The town was a well-known seaside resort. They walked along the sand until they came to a deserted spot where the man emptied the chair of its contents and flopped himself down in it. "This is just the spot for our experiment. Fetch driftwood and make a pile of it just here." Jack did as he was told.

Taking the magnifying glass, the Practical Man held it over the pile and a tiny sun appeared on one of the sticks, getting hotter and hotter, until, with a PUFF! it burst into flame.

"The Sun's arrived!" cried the Practical Man, pulling a toasting fork from inside his jacket. "Now, my little beauty, jump in." With the sting of the toasting fork in his rump, Jack jumped …

AT HIGH TEA

WAVE QUENCH FIRE

FIRE BOIL KETTLE

AT HIGH TIDE

At this point, Sir Isaac Newton himself enters the story. By now he is very old and grey, and some of his less good theories have been disproved by the clever men of today, but despite all, his Universal Law of Gravitation still rules everywhere.

Although the Moon had disobeyed his laws, and would therefore have to forfeit the Hare-bell, it seemed unfair that the brave little hare should end up toasted by the Practical Man. Besides, although this may not be the happiest of stories, it is not a tragedy.

When he saw Jack Hare jump towards the fire, and the Practical Man brandishing the toasting fork, Sir Isaac grabbed the strings of gravitational force that bound Jack to his destiny and PULLED —————

Jack was deflected mid-leap, swerved sideways and fell SPLASH into the water. This now completed the Moon's curious instructions. He'd started in the earth, had gone up into the air with Tara Tree-tops, had passed through the fire of the Practical Man, and now here he was in the water.

Down and down he fell into the gloomy depths, until he could hardly see a paw in front of his face.

Then, through the murky waters, he saw a distant yellow light. This must surely be the Sun, thought Jack. To find out what he really saw, answer this slippery riddle:

> My first begins first, and I am myself my second. My next is the end of ends, followed by the beginning of hope.
> Now put me on one line, and you will find my name,
> I live my whole life out of doors, but never feel the rain.

JACK QUICK

AND JACK JUMPS

JACK BE NIMBLE

OVER THE FLAME

Jack could see now that it wasn't the Sun after all. "Glood day," said the fish, sounding like someone with a mouthful of cherries.

"Oh," said Jack, "I thought you were my Sun."

"How abslurd."

"No, no," said Jack, "the SUN," and drew a big circle in the water.

"Then why have you come to the blottom of the ocean?"

Dear me, thought Jack, this is going to take all day. I'll flatter him. "Please, oh fish, most worthy, noble and glorious fish, please, fishy most high, can you direct me to the Sun?"

"You've blissed out educated," said the fish conceitedly, "blut I will help you if you can blanswer this riddle:

> "What is nothing on its outside,
> And nothing on its inside,
> Is lighter than a fleather,
> But ten men cannot pick it up?"

Jack opened his mouth and out came a bubble! "Correct," said the fish. "Now flollow the frog. He will show you where lives the Spirit of Water. She will tell you how to get to the Sun."

Jack followed the frog and they swam until they came to a sparkling lake, where a charming young lady swam back and forth, measuring its length.

"Next time she passes," said the frog, "ask her."

Jack did, and this was her strange reply:

"Stand at the water's edge a little before the Sun sets in the west, and you will see a yellow carpet. If you can run its length before the Sun has time to set, you will reach your destination. Good luck!"

I AM HYDROGEN

CRYSTAL

Already the golden light of late afternoon was colouring the sky, and Jack realised that time was getting short. So, running as fast as his legs would carry him, he set off for the West Country. With not a minute to spare, he reached the shore, and there, spread out over the sea between him and the Sun, was a bright yellow pathway. Without stopping, not even to take breath, the hare LEAPED.

Jack travelled so speedily and reached such a velocity that Sir Isaac Newton and his gravity were forced to let him go. He had now escaped the earth's powerful attraction, and was travelling end over end, through space towards the Sun.

Sir Isaac looked out over the sea and said to himself, "All my life I seem to have been only like a boy playing on the sea-shore and diverting myself in now and then finding a smoother pebble or a prettier shell than ordinary, whilst the great ocean of truth lay all undiscovered before me."

On reaching the Sun, Jack was horrified to find that he no longer had the jewel ... IT WAS GONE!

"Well," said the Sun, with a loud commanding voice, "why have you come here?"

Jack thought quickly, then said, "Great Lord Sun, I bring you a precious gift from a noble and gracious lady, and it would be yours if it were not the answer to this riddle:

> "Fifty is my first,
> Nothing is my second,
> A snake will make my third,
> Then three parts a cross is reckoned.
> Now to find my name, fit my parts together,
> I am all your past, and you fear me in cold weather?"

THE SUN SET AND THE DAY WAS OVER.

Dear Reader,

If you were to read this book again, you might discover when and where the hare lost the jewel. If you do, then go and find it, and keep it for yourself, but remember:

The best of men is only a man at best,
And a hare, as everyone knows, is only a hare.

First published by Schocken Books 1980
First American edition

Second printing, November 1980

© 1979 by Kit Williams

Library of Congress Cataloging in Publication Data
Williams, Kit.
Masquerade.
Reprint of the ed. published by J. Cape, London.
I. Title.
PZ4.W726295Mas 1980   [PR6073.I43227]
823'.914   80–14127

Manufactured in the United States of America

Printed by A. Hoen & Co.
Bound by Keenan Binders, Inc.

Kit William's original works of art are exhibited
exclusively by Portal Gallery Ltd., London,
England.

JOHN OF GOD

JOHN OF GOD

THE BRAZILIAN HEALER WHO'S
TOUCHED THE LIVES OF MILLIONS

HEATHER CUMMING AND KAREN LEFFLER

FOREWORD BY
AMIT GOSWAMI, PH.D.

ATRIA BOOKS
New York London Toronto Sydney

ATRIA BOOKS
1230 Avenue of the Americas
New York, NY 10020

BEYOND WORDS
PUBLISHING
20827 N.W. Cornell Road, Suite 500
Hillsboro, Oregon 97124-9808
503-531-8700
503-531-8773 fax
www.beyondword.com

Editor: Jessica Bryan
Managing editor: Henry Covi
Proofreader: Marvin Moore
Cover and interior design: Carol Sibley
Composition: William H. Brunson Typography Services

First Atria Books / Beyond Words hardcover edition May 2007

ATRIA BOOKS is a trademark of Simon & Schuster, Inc.

Beyond Words Publishing is a division of Simon & Schuster, Inc.

For more information about special discounts for bulk purchases, please contact Simon & Schuster Special Sales at 1-800-456-6798 or business@simonandschuster.com.

Manufactured in the United States of America

10 9 8 7 6 5 4 3 2 1

Library of Congress Cataloging-in-Publication Data

Cumming, Heather.
    John of God : the brazilian healer who's touched the lives of millions / Heather Cumming and Karen Leffler. — 1st Atria Books/Beyond Words hardcover ed.
        p.   cm.
    Includes bibliographical references
        1. Faria, João Teixeira da.   2. Spiritual healing and spiritualism—Brazil.   3. Psychic surgery—Brazil.   I. Leffler, Karen.   II. Title.

BF1275.F3C86   2007
615.8'52092—dc22
[B]
                                                                2006038321

ISBN-13: 978-1-58270-164-6 (hardcover)
ISBN-10:   1-58270-164-4 (hardcover)

The corporate mission of Beyond Words Publishing, Inc.: *Inspire to Integrity*

I have listened and I have looked with open eyes.
I have poured my soul into the world seeking the unknown within the known.
*And I sing out loud in amazement.**
—Rabindranath Tagore, Indian mystic and poet (1861–1941)

*As paraphrased by Amit Goswami in *The Self-Aware Universe.*

We dedicate this book to Medium João Teixeira de Faria, fondly known as "John of God," and the phalange of compassionate, evolved spirits who work at the Casa de Dom Inácio de Loyola in Abadiânia, Brazil. Their dedication to service and love of humanity is indeed fathomless. Lastly, we dedicate this book to the awakening Spirit in each of us.

For one man to commit his life to the healing of the collective society without asking for adulation of any kind speaks volumes to his gentle humility. Our prayer, our book, our song is in response to this amazing gift that the Divine Spirit has given us here on earth.

May this book, in a small way, reflect back to Medium João and the guiding spirits our immense love and gratitude for healings that are beyond measure.

Thank You

Heather Cumming   Karen Leffler

CONTENTS

PREFACE

Neither of us had ever entertained the idea that we would write a book about John of God, but in the winter of 2003, the Entity told us, "Not only should you write a book, you must!" And so began our work of documenting testimonials of the remarkable healings that occurred at the Casa. As Heather gathered stories, spirit photos materialized for Karen. It seemed a perfect union of energies and skills. When Sebastian, the secretary of the Casa, heard what we were doing, he, too, shared a wealth of stories. Soon the book began to fall into place.

Our work has shown us that most, if not all, visitors to the Casa experience unconditional love for the first time when they meet the Entities. This first encounter is profound and not adequately captured by a secondhand narrative of the experience. And yet words are all we have to convey the emotions experienced by those who have been to the Casa. So, in this book you will read miraculous stories in the very words of people who have experienced healings; it offers a window into the hearts of those touched and healed by the loving and compassionate Entities. And if words are not enough, you will also see the physical manifestations of spirit energy—revealed to us with their permission—in various photographs taken at the Casa.

After visiting the Casa, many people say their lives have changed; rather than *talk* of love their goal is to *live* life from love. Their personal experiences remind us that divinity is a work in progress. The Casa offers several spiritual tools toward this endeavor. Judgment and criticism are surrendered to forgiveness, tolerance, respect, caring through good works, and dedication to live life authentically, as our true selves. We have been given so much by the Entities, our divine guides, family, and friends. Their support and encouragement has been immense, and we are extremely grateful for the blessings.

It is our hope that this book will introduce you to the work of John of God and the Casa. By reading this book you will have opened the door to this work in your life—whether you visit the Casa or not. It is our hope that the blessings we have received will also be a part of your experience as well.

Brazilians have a saying that God was inspired when He created Brazil; we wholeheartedly agree. And we believe God was exceptionally inspired when bringing Medium João Teixeira de Faria into the world.

INTRODUCTION

The Entity (Dr. José Valdivino) called for his instruments again. I opened the special drawer and carefully removed the tray and took the instrument tray to him. He chose a paring knife, a regular kitchen serrated-edged knife. He passed his hand over the man's eye and told him to relax. He opened the eye wide and pressed down hard and scraped. "See, here it is," he said, as he wiped the knife on the man's shirt. I could see a minute dark sliver. I know beyond a doubt after seeing so many of these operations that the sliver was not a topical foreign object being removed, but rather something from deep inside that only the Entities can see. The Entity looks into the eye as a representation of the whole body system not limited to the physical eye. I understand this as a symbolic removal on the physical level, but originating from many levels and involving many different organs. "O filho esta curado pode levar" (The son is healed. You can take him to the infirmary), he said, as he wrote the post-op prescription ...

—from Heather's journal

As a full *trance-medium*, Medium João becomes like a hollow reed. He leaves his body in complete trust to the care of disembodied spirits called Entities, all of whom were remarkable people during their own physical lives. This form of embodiment of a living person by another spirit is known as *incorporation*. These transcendent spirits are able to use Medium João's body to produce cures by performing visible and invisible spiritual surgeries. Medium João can incorporate approximately thirty-seven Entities, but only one Entity can be incorporated at a time. This specific Entity may change, however, depending upon the needs of an individual patient. In addition to the Entity incorporated at any given time, there is a highly evolved group of thousands of spirits who actually work on a person while the incorporated Entity oversees the healing. This group is referred to as his *phalange*. One spirit might specialize in diabetes or heart problems, another in emotional afflictions. These Entities serve humanity in the hopes of alleviating pain and suffering on the earthly plane. This service is part of *their* evolutionary process. John of God has fulfilled his mission as a *medium* for over forty-eight years (since approximately 1958) and has participated in the healing of over eight million people.

People who have been seen by the Entities are continually guided and protected thereafter. Their lives begin to be a part of the current of divine love flowing from the Entities. This current cleans them like a mirror is cleaned to give a perfect reflection. Visitors to the Casa simply ask for help, and it is given. It is a great revelation to realize that there are literally thousands of spirits working in collaboration with the immense dedication of John of God to alleviate the suffering of humanity. It is difficult to conceive of such kindness enveloping and healing each person simply because they have sincerely asked for it. This is the beginning of true faith, which, in turn, naturally evolves into the desire to serve others.

WHAT'S IN A NAME?

There are many different "voices" in this book because the authors have included interviews of many of the people associated with John of God and his work at the Casa, including friends and business partners from his hometown, Casa volunteers, and those who come from around the world for healing.

Throughout the book, the entities incorporated by John of God are sometimes named by the person speaking. In these instances, the name of the Entity is shown in parentheses—for example, "the Entity (Dr. Augusto)." When the specific spirit being incorporated is not known, only "the Entity" is used. When the meaning is obvious, only the name of the Entity is given.

João Teixeira de Faria is commonly referred to as "John of God" by thousands of people from around the world, although João, the man, does not care for this name. He prefers to be called "Medium João." Spoken of here in a more general way, he is called "John of God." He is referred to as "the Entity" or "Pai Father" when he incorporates. Karen, Heather, and others close to him also call him "Medium João."

The Entities and Medium João often use the term *filho*, which is masculine and means "son," and *filha*, which is feminine and means "daughter." The terms "children" and "children of the Casa" are also used. These affectionate terms are meant in the sense of our kinship with one another in our common search for spiritual growth.

John of God has authorized and participated fully in the writing of this book about his life and mission, the Entities, and the Casa. He has contributed numerous insights and details—beginning with Chapter I, which tells the story of his youth, his poverty, and his eventual discovery of his full trance-mediumship.

In Chapter 2, the authors describe a visit to Itapaçi, the birth home of John of God. In this chapter, he shares a day in his remarkable life and gives a videotaped interview, during which he incorporates and the Entity speaks.

Chapter 3 contains a beautiful and poignant interview with Ana Keyla Teixeira Lorenço, the wife of Medium João. Ana opens her heart and speaks about her husband and his life as a medium. She gives us a glimpse into the man and his mission as well as wonderful insights about the Casa.

In Chapter 4, readers will be acquainted with Brazil and given a brief overview of a trip to Abadiânia, the village in the plateau region of central Brazil where John of God's healing center is located. This chapter includes contributions by Casa volunteers and mediums.

Chapters 5, 6, and 7 offer an in-depth look at the Casa so readers can experience it for themselves. Chapter 8 recounts an amazing trip with John of God to Peru. Spiritism and the Entities are discussed in Chapter 9, including background information about the lives of some of the Entities. *Spiritualism* is a movement that believes the spirits of the dead can communicate with the living through a medium, a person who functions as a *channel* for communication. *Spiritism* is a collection of principles and spiritual laws based on the teachings of Jesus. There are more centers for the study of Spiritism in Brazil than anywhere else on Earth.

Chapter 10 contains miraculous healing stories contributed by visitors to the Casa, followed by the afterword and the bibliography and suggested reading. Many rare photographs of John of God are shown in the photo sections of the book, including the incredible spirit photographs taken by Karen Leffler.

Dr. Amit Goswami has said, "Everything starts with consciousness," and we see the Casa as a working model, living proof of how consciousness is fundamental to the Universe. We actively engage in our own healing through our free will by our intention to offer ourselves to this Consciousness for healing and spiritual growth. When viewed in this way, the healing that occurs is not miraculous but simply a part of a scientific paradigm.

FOREWORD

John of God is more than a person; he is a scientific phenomenon of utmost importance, and so I wish to supplement the authors' loving and beautiful exposition of the phenomenon that is John of God with a scientific explanation.

In our search for meaning, every now and then two individuals' searches converge and these individuals become correlated. Quantum physics, when properly interpreted within the primacy of consciousness, makes it possible to explain such correlation as an aspect of quantum nonlocality. Quantum nonlocality involves signalless communication that takes place via the interconnectedness called consciousness, which connects us outside of space and time; hence no signal is needed for such communication. You can call people with the capacity for nonlocal communication psychics, but beware! We all potentially have this capacity. The phenomenon behind John of God is special because it corresponds to a rather unusual rendering of this capacity. In John of God's case, one communicator, John of God (aka, Medium João) is incarnate—he has a physical body—but the other communicator is discarnate without any physical body.

So the scientific explanation of the phenomenon of John of God involves such questions as, Can there be discarnate entities? Can a living person communicate with a discarnate entity? How is the scientific proof determined?

Well, dear reader, brace yourself. All these questions can be addressed and answered scientifically. In this book you will read about a scientifically credible, albeit controversial, phenomenon. You will also read about healing through unconditional love, and that, too, has a scientific explanation.

If you talk with old-paradigm scientists—those avowed subscribers to the philosophy of scientific materialism that considers all phenomena as manifestations of matter—they will assert that talking about a discarnate entity smacks of dualism. "Any interaction requires exchange of energy, and energy of the physical world is never lost. How do such discarnate, presumably nonphysical, entities interact with a physical entity such as a medium?" they will ask smugly.

Is there an answer to dualism? In quantum physics, all objects are quantum possibilities. It is our experience of material objects that gives them the material qualities which we sense with our sensory organs. This opens up the question of other possibilities that can be experienced differently: not through senses.

The paradigm-shifting metaphysics that quantum physics requires us to subscribe to (otherwise, we get bogged down with unsolvable paradoxes of logic) is that consciousness is the ground of all being. In this ground, other quantum possibilities coexist with material possibilities for consciousness to choose from in order to create experiences other than sensing. We all have experiences of feeling vital energies, thinking about mental meaning, and intuiting value/archetypes, such as love, beauty, truth, and justice. There is no dualism in consciousness interacting with the physical, mental, vital, and archetypal worlds because these worlds are possibilities of consciousness itself from which consciousness chooses to make manifest experiences. Our vital energies, mental meanings, and intuitive archetypes are nonphysical, no doubt, but their interaction with the physical is mediated by consciousness. Therefore, again, no dualism is involved.

In this way, we possess not only a physical body but also a subtle psyche consisting of vital, mental, and archetypal components, which are all embodied within consciousness. Can we survive the death of the physical body? Yes, the subtle bodies survive along with their ground, consciousness itself. Yes, discarnate existence is possible!

A detailed theoretical investigation tells us several things:[1]

1. Although the vital and mental worlds do not have structures like the physical world has, as we live life, our experiences of living produce a functional modification of the vital and mental possibilities that we use most often, giving us functional vital and mental bodies that correlate with the physical. Thus, not only is there survival after the death of the physical, but also individuality in what survives. In contrast to physical memory, which dies with the physical body, there are subtle quantum memories contained within our vital and mental bodies. These memories survive and can even be recalled in future incarnations. When that happens, we get reincarnation. I call the entity that survives and reincarnates a *quantum monad.*

2. What survives then is not the history part of our ego but what we call character, our tendencies and habit patterns.

3. However, conscious choice from possibility to actual events of experience requires the physical body. So the discarnate

1. As outlined in my book *Physics of the Soul.*

existence after death is devoid of ongoing experiences. Materialists can relax; this is not like a Hollywood movie!

4. But if a material body is available, what then? Suppose an incarnate person, a medium, by prior nonlocal agreement related to meaning-processing, periodically allows a discarnate quantum monad to use his or her physical body to produce experience! This is how mediumistic communication, or channeling, takes place (called incorporation in this book).

5. If this model is correct, then during channeling both mental and vital characters of the channeler would be replaced by different mental and vital character. A different mental character would be indicated best by a different set of mental expertise or skill. A different vital character would be indicated by not only different sets of vital skills but also by the ability to function within a new range of many physiological parameters.

Medium João channels the quantum memory of someone else, who lived before and died. Indeed, while John of God channels, he abruptly transforms his character to radiate unconditional love that heals those who need healing.

What is the evidence that Medium João—John of God's character—really changes so drastically that it can stand up to scientific challenge? Heather Cumming and Karen Leffler have done well in documenting and reporting, often with photographs, in order to prove beyond any reasonable doubt that medium João acquires extraordinary abilities when he incorporates or channels a discarnate entity.

▲ Medium João was never trained as a doctor, let alone as a surgeon. Yet, when he channels a suitable entity, he successfully performs surgery on patients of varying ailments.

▲ Medium João's manners, stance, and speech all change when he incorporates. He emanates love that others can feel.

▲ Perhaps the most impressive piece of evidence reported in the book occurred when John of God had a stroke that paralyzed one side of his body. First, during this period, strangely whenever John of God channeled an Entity, he behaved normally; he had no paralysis. Second, and even more strangely, medium João was able to channel an entity and operate on himself. He recovered from this paralytic condition and remains healthy to this day. Third, medium João normally is sickened and faints at the sight of blood, but that did not happen during this event when he performed surgery on himself under incorporation. This remains true in other instances of channeling and surgery by Medium João as well.

The authors report that there is now an elaborate healing protocol developed around Medium João that allows anybody to come and be healed. The protocol in which other mediums assist John of God typically resembles prayer and (vital) energy healing, except that mediumship and channeling are involved. There is now considerable understanding of prayer healing as quantum healing—self-healing through quantum leaps from our separate suffering ego to holistic states of our consciousness. A quantum leap is a discontinuous transition. Indeed, there are many instances where the healing is instantaneous, thus supporting this view.[2]

In truth, although quantum healing requires a quantum leap, it is often imperative that the patient undergoes a protracted creative process consisting of four stages: preparation or "work," relaxation or "surrender to being," sudden quantum leap of insight, and manifestation. In the healing that takes place in John of God's casa, often the patients have to go through a process of preparation and surrender before the quantum leap of healing takes place.

2. See my book *The Quantum Doctor* for further details on the subject.

The primary message of this foreword is that the John of God phenomenon is entirely credible from the new "science-within-consciousness" point of view. But I don't want to leave the impression that this book about John of God is only important for science. The truth is, it will inspire many people to experiment with the energies of love and the healing power that is available to all of us. I have researched this subject myself, both intellectually and experientially, and I submit that the Entities who communicate through John of God are available to every one. Commonly, such an Entity is called a *spirit guide*. The creative power of quantum healing is also available to each of us provided we are willing to go through the creative process.

Finally, I want to say that although I have not met John of God personally, the authors have created such a wonder-filled and loving exposition about him that after reading their book I feel I know Medium João, I feel the unconditional love of the Entities who communicate through him. If you read this book, I believe you will feel the same inspiration.

What more can I say? Here in this book is a manifestation of the energies of love happening locally in Brazil, and Heather and Karen have made it possible to share these energies globally from elsewhere and anywhere! For this I am grateful, and I hope you will be, too.

Amit Goswami, Ph.D.

THE BOY, THE MAN, THE MEDIUM

I am the happiest man in the world because God entrusted me with this mission.

—João Teixeira de Faria

João Teixeira de Faria was born of humble origins in the village of Cachoeira da Fumaça, in the State of Goiás, central Brazil. His mother, Francisca Teixeira Damas, was known to all as *Dona Iuca*. She was a hardworking housewife, dedicated to the upbringing of her children and well liked and respected by all who knew her. João is very proud of his mother and speaks of her with great love and admiration. In the 1940s and '50s, there were no paved roads or infrastructure in this part of Brazil. The roads connecting the towns were dirt, studded with cattle grids, and wound their way through farms and villages. When construction of paved roads began in the late 1950s, João's mother ran a small hotel and cooked for the road workers to augment her family's meager income. João often says his mother became famous for her delicious cooking. His father, Jose Nunes de Faria, known as *Juca Faria*, made his living as a tailor and owned a laundry service. He struggled unsuccessfully to support his family. João, the youngest, had four brothers: Americano, José, Francisco, and Abilio; and one sister, America.

His brothers have all passed. His sister lives in Anápolis and is now eighty-three years old.

João was brought up in the town of Itapaçi, also in Goiás State. Itapaçi is roughly 170 kilometers (105 miles) from Abadiânia, where the Casa de Dom Inácio de Loyola is now located. João, or *John*, the name he was known by as a boy, began working as a cloth cutter in his father's tailor shop at the age of six to help supplement his father's scant income. At this young age, he was already learning the trade that would eventually sustain his spiritual mission. Before the social reforms of the 1960s, it was very common for children living in the interior of Brazil to leave school after only a few years of education. They were needed to earn a living by tending cattle and other livestock, carrying lunches on horseback to workers in the fields, and working in brick factories. They usually began learning a trade by the time they were eight or nine years old.

João attended primary school at Grupo Escolar Santa Teresinha in Itapaçi, but after two years poverty forced him to abandon his studies and go to work. He has toiled as a well digger, a bricklayer, and in many other kinds of hard manual labor. João never resumed his studies, and to this day he can neither read nor write. Yes, this brilliant, natural clairvoyant earned pocket money to go to the pool hall by accurately prophesizing events. All that João remembers of this experience is coming back from "flying." After being given money, he would return to the pool hall. He is an excellent pool player to this day. He also remembers walking into the fields with the villagers and pointing to roots and plants that would heal their ailments.

The first recorded occasion of João's paranormal abilities took place when he was nine years old while he was visiting family in the town of Nova Ponte with his mother. It was a beautiful cloudless day, but João had a premonition that a huge storm was coming. He began pointing out houses, including the houses of his brother, and saying they would be blown down or would lose their roofs. He urged his mother to leave before the storm. Although she was not convinced, she humored her son and they sought refuge in a friend's home nearby. Exactly as he had predicted, the thunderstorm appeared, seemingly out of nowhere, and badly damaged or destroyed about forty houses in a small town of approximately 150 dwellings.

Work was scarce in Itapaçi, and João was forced out into the world in search of employment. His life was difficult as he moved from town to town working manual-labor jobs. One day when he was at Campo Grande, in the State of Mato Grosso, far from home, João became hungry, tired, and lonely—and unemployed once again. Saddened and weak from hunger, he sought refuge under a bridge on the outskirts of town. He planned to bathe in the river before continuing his search for work. As he approached the water's edge, a beautiful woman called out to him. She invited him to come closer, and they spent a memorable afternoon in conversation. The following morning, remembering the beauty and gentleness of the young woman, he was drawn back to the river to talk with her again. He was astounded to find a brilliant shaft of light where she had been seated. He was further amazed to hear her voice beckoning to him by name.

She told João to go to the Spiritist Center of Christ the Redeemer. He followed her explicit guidance, and when he arrived, the director of the Center approached and asked him if his name was "João Teixeira de Faria." The director said they knew he was coming and had been waiting for him. At that very moment, João fainted. When he returned to consciousness, hours later, he was embarrassed and most apologetic, attributing his fainting spell to hunger. There was a large group of people surrounding him, and someone told him that he had incorporated the Entity King Solomon, and over fifty people had been cured thereafter. The congregation was enthralled with his mediumship and the healing that had transpired.

João thought of himself as merely another impoverished teenager. He was confused by all the attention. He insisted he had done nothing, repeating that he had only fainted and did not know what they were talking about. The director, sensitive to the young boy's bafflement, gently took him aside. He explained that an Entity of Light known as King Solomon had asked João to return promptly at 2:00 P.M. the following day to resume the work. Furthermore, the director said, he would be honored to have João stay the night at his house so they could talk about the day's events and other spiritual matters.

The director drove João to his home and had ample but simple food prepared. It was an elaborate meal for João, who had not eaten in many days. After dinner, he was given his own room with a revolving fan and a mosquito net. He had never known such luxury. The next morning, following another wonderful meal, he thought, *I better eat all I can, while I can, because I'm sure they will send me away soon.*

João returned to the Center with his host, explaining nervously that he was not a practicing medium, nor did he have any understanding of medicine or the spiritual world. He had no explanation for what had taken place the previous day. He was actually terrified because he did not understand what was expected of him at 2:00 P.M. After the group had gathered and the opening prayer ended, João incorporated King Solomon once more and the work of healing the sick began.

An intense period of spiritual instruction and guidance by the Entities followed over the next few months. Medium João, as he now began to be called, was directed to dedicate his life to healing others. João was sixteen years of age when he had this first experience of mediumship. Poverty had forced him out into the world in search of employment, but it had also served to bring him to his mission. In Mato Grosso, he found his true purpose: to serve God and humanity.

He later realized that the beautiful woman at the waters' edge was the spirit of St. Rita de Cascia.

When Heather asked Medium João what St. Rita had said to him that day, he replied, "Love and believe in a higher being, which is God. I have always been a devout follower of Saint Rita of Cascia. She communicated to me at length that day as a brilliant shaft of light, and I was guided on many spiritual matters."

Over the next five or six years, Medium João traveled throughout Brazil consoling the suffering, healing the sick, and counseling all those who came to him. During those early days, he was known as *João Curador* (John the Healer); however, he still refuses to be called a *curandeiro* (healer) or *milagreiro* (miracle worker).

While practicing his extraordinary work of healing the sick during the early years, Medium João was persecuted by members of the medical and religious establishments, who were threatened by his presence in their towns. He has lost count of the times he was arrested and accused of practicing clandestine medicine. Constantly pursued, he was always seeking refuge from the authorities.

Brazil suffered a revolution in 1962, and a military government came into power. By 1964, the new capital, Brasília, had been established. João went there to offer his services as a tailor to the military. Because he was so young, he was not commissioned to create uniforms but was given an opportunity to sew a consignment of work pants. His expertise impressed his new employers, and he was soon promoted to full-time tailor and assigned to make uniforms for the army.

Medium João continued his healing work quietly on the side, but word of his gift soon spread throughout the barracks. One day, he incorporated an Entity who operated on the wounded leg of a doctor, which healed immediately. The doctor was enthralled with Medium João's gift, and from that day on, he became the spiritual healer for the military and civil authorities. He was promoted to master tailor and became their protégé for nearly nine years. Consequently, he was protected from persecution during that time and traveled extensively throughout Brazil with the army.

These formative years greatly influenced João and created a burning passion inside of him to become a successful businessman. He needed moneymaking expertise to support his spiritual purpose. His beginning fame brought business opportunities, and he took advantage of them. He has since become a cattle farmer and miner. João has an innate gift for business and has invested wisely, which affords him the ability to concentrate on his dedicated mission of alleviating suffering and helping the poor. Although Medium João has made a promise to the Entities that he will never charge for his services, the Casa gratefully accepts donations.

Although many businessmen, lawyers, and politicians agree that John of God is an extremely intelligent and astute businessman, he is saddened by his lack of formal education. Many times he has been moved to tears when admitting that he cannot even write a check. He had wanted to study and perhaps become a lawyer. Yet, when asked if he has endured a difficult life, he adamantly denies any suffering and affirms that he has been blessed from birth.

2

A DAY IN THE LIFE OF JOÃO, THE MAN

For those who believe, no words are necessary;
for those who do not believe, no words are possible.

—Dom Inácio de Loyola

In February 2005, Karen knelt before the Entity, grateful for the profound love and blessings she had received. He gently held her hand as the tears began to roll softly down her cheeks. She was returning to America in two days. He said to her, "Vai com a bença de Deus, filha" (Go with the blessings of God, daughter). Then he turned to Heather and said, "What are you doing tomorrow, Filha Heather? Would you like to take 150 people down to the waterfall?"

"Karen and I are planning to go to Itapaçi, Medium João's hometown, to take photographs for the book," Heather responded.

He chewed on the cap of the ballpoint pen he used to write prescriptions. We thought he might be incorporated as the Entity Dr. Valdivino. This is a trait we have noticed when Dr. Valdivino is contemplating. "Good," he said. "Medium João will be there tomorrow. I will ask somebody else to take the filhos to the waterfall."

Later that day, Maninho, a taxi driver, told us that Medium João had asked him to drive us to his house at 6:00 A.M. the following day, because Medium João would like to accompany us to Itapaçi. We were thrilled at this opportunity to spend the day with Maninho, Medium João, and his wife, Ana. We expected it would be a revealing glimpse into the family life of this extraordinary man.

We arose on Saturday with the roosters and went directly to Anápolis where Medium João lives. In our excitement, we were an hour early, so we stopped at Joaquim's house. We had promised to take him with us to visit his mother in Itapaçi. During his youth, Joaquim and his mother had laundered and delivered clothes for João's tailoring business. Now Joaquim works at the Casa and sells delicious coconut desserts. As is the hospitality of Brazil, Joaquim insisted we sit for a moment and have hot, sweet *cafézinho* (sweet black coffee) before leaving.

We were embarrassed to call and disturb Medium João so early, but then the phone rang and it was him calling to chide us. "It's 6:00 A.M. Where are you?" We agreed to meet him on the road in the car with Maninho and Joaquim. True to his word, about 7:00 A.M., a large pickup truck roared past us with the horn honking. Ana was at his side. He waved for us to follow as he pulled his truck off the road at a coconut stand. Our glorious day had begun. He knew the old woman who owned the stand and told us about her husband, who had been treated by the Entities for many years and had now passed over. Medium João never drives past her stand without stopping to buy a sack of coconuts and visit with her. He cut open an unripe, green coconut for each of us, and we sat at a table at the roadside shack sipping the delicately-flavored juice. The whitish, filmy liquid is neither sweet nor tart and is laden with minerals. Medium João reminded us of the healing properties of this drink, which is prescribed by doctors in Brazil for dehydration.

Our next stop was a half hour away at the watermelon stand. He carefully chose a watermelon for us by rapping his knuckles on different ones until he heard the proper hollow sound. Cutting open the perfect melon, he handed large slices to each of us. We leaned forward as the sweet juice dripped all over our hands, clothes, and onto the dirt floor. He kept feeding us more and more slices. As his wife, Ana, says, "It is impossible to be on a diet around Medium João. Not only does he love food, but he is always the generous host. For him, an essential ingredient of good hospitality is food and plenty of it. He is also a great cook."

He left the watermelon stand behind in a cloud of dust, and we followed behind him. It was a three-hour drive to our destination, and keeping up with him was a challenge. We stopped again on the outskirts of Itapaçi. Medium João brought us to a simple adobe house with dirt floors and many chickens running free. An elderly man greeted us and led us to his vegetable garden. He told Medium João to help himself. We watched as Medium João enthusiastically cut the vegetables with his penknife. For today, he was far from the enormous responsibilities of the Casa. He unloaded an armful of vegetables into a basket for the old man to price.

The man exclaimed, "I know you. You are João de Deus (John of God). I took my wife to you. It must be twenty years ago. You look good, just the same."

Medium João put his arm around the man. "How is she?" he said. "Was she healed?"

The man called his wife over. "God bless you. I was completely healed," she said.

Medium João walked over to a rooster and two chickens, which were confined to a small crate, and asked to purchase them. The chickens were to be taken to his farm and set loose with his breeding stock.

Karen had been taking photographs since we left Abadiânia. When Medium João had held up freshly picked scallions a few moments before, spirit light was clearly recorded next to him.

When Karen took a photo showing him opening the crate, and another of Maninho grabbing the chickens, three distinct white globes could be seen floating above the crate.

From a shamanic point of view, Heather wonders if the three globes of light depicted the soul loss of the chickens. The trauma of being trapped in a cage could have been exacerbated. It is similar to a person recounting a car accident. People sometimes say they were able to observe themselves from a distance after an accident. Part of their consciousness may have left their body at the moment of impact, enabling them to see the traumatic scene. According to shamanism, this is a survival mechanism known as *soul loss*. It can be experienced by both animals and humans.

We drove through Itapaçi, a pretty little town with tree-lined boulevards and old churches. Medium João pulled up to his parent's home and pointed to three simple houses in a quiet family neighborhood. Walking over to the smallest structure, he put his hand on the wall and said proudly, "This is where I was brought up. Karen, take a photograph. Of course it did not look like this then. Over the years I was able to buy this home and construct the other two for my mother and brother."

Pacu and Oswaldo Moura Machado embraced Medium João. They were all friends from childhood. Medium João hugged each of them fondly, and then said, "This man came from a much better background than I. When we first met, my father was very poor, and we barely had a roof over our heads. I began working in my father's tailor shop at the age of six. Pacu and I fetched and delivered laundry for him. Thank God I am known throughout Brazil now and have been able to travel to many countries in the world. Without the Grace of God, none of this would have been possible. I would not have been able to buy this land. And I say, even with everything I have, I am the owner of nothing. The rightful owner of all that I have is God. I am fulfilling my mission here, and God has given me more than I could ever have dreamed."

Medium João's brother, Francisco, had died the previous month, and Medium João was planning to spend the weekend with his-sister-in law, Neusa, as well as show us his home. He ushered us into her covered porch and introduced us. She was preparing lunch by an open log range. Her home was a simple dwelling: small rooms with white walls. The sparse living room displayed pictures of Medium João, the family, and his beloved mother. The three houses were interconnected by a shared courtyard and one tiled verandah. Over the years, the house had become somewhat dilapidated. In the corner were a cold-water tub and a laundry scrub board, fundamental components of rural Brazilian homes.

Ana quickly set to work washing the freshly picked vegetables and preparing snacks. She flatly refused all assistance and kept us amused with lively conversation. Meanwhile, Medium João sat back, relaxing in the environment he so loves. He introduced us to his friends:

"This young man is Pacu's son. He has worked for me on my farms and on many projects. He is a builder and bricklayer. He works hard to earn a living. He is going to remodel my brother's house, where my sister-in-law will continue to live. My background is not what people think. We were very poor. My origins are from here. I am proud of my roots and keep in touch with my friends from the past."

Medium João put money in Maninho's pocket and asked him to run to the store to pick up onions, garlic, green peppers, and two and half kilos of tomatoes. "But please, make sure the tomatoes are really ripe. Hurry, we don't want to go hungry. I am going to cook for all of us." Medium João took us over to the outside stove, which had been stoked with large pieces of wood. He prepared to cook on the grate above the open fire as is typically done in Brazil. Pouring a great deal of oil into a large pan, he added garlic and white rice, a staple at every meal. Smoke billowed out all around us as he stirred the rice. "Do you like to cook?" he asked

11

us. "I love cooking. You'll see I am a good cook. I especially love cooking on these old open log ranges. Hey, chief, bring the water."

Medium João went over to the water basin and washed the pork ribs while continuing to chat with us. "I've always been a good cook, haven't I, Joaquim? I cooked for you when you were a kid. The real way to cook this dish is not by sautéing the pork but by curing the pork with salt and spices and letting it cook in the sun. After several days, the sun-cured pork meat is added to the chicken. It gives a wonderful flavor. Heather, tell everyone they are liberated to eat the pork and chilies today. And, by the way, the water coming out of these faucets has been energized just like the Casa water. You can eat and drink everything here. Nothing will harm you."

We spent a wonderful afternoon eating the food that Medium João had prepared for us. People had heard by word of mouth that he was in Itapaçi, and a steady stream of visitors came to pay their respects or seek help. One particular minister paid inappropriate attention to Medium João's sister-in-law and pressured Medium João for money for his ministry. Medium João diplomatically and skillfully defended his sister-in-law, and the man left quickly.

We withdrew to the tile veranda. A young boy came by selling popsicles in a little cooler. His success was assured for the day when Medium João bought the whole stock and sent him off for more. Ana certainly has a hard time keeping Medium João on a diet. Both the Entities and the medical doctors have put him on a strict diet, but he rarely adheres to it.

Following Medium João's example, we all lay down on the cool tile and took a brief siesta. A rooster, who had escaped and was clambering over fences and rooftops, abruptly awakened us. Medium João jumped up and took chase with Maninho. It was great sport, and they returned victorious.

We spent the rest of the afternoon sitting on the tile floor talking with Medium João. He teased us and told wonderful stories—

some of which were made up just for fun. It was impossible not to laugh, and the more we did, the more it encouraged him. Heather, having spent much of her life in the interior of Brazil, was reminded of the lazy afternoons of her youth on the farm when she sat and talked with the wranglers and their families.

As we prepared to take our leave so Medium João and Ana could enjoy a quiet evening together, he sat up and said, "Interview these two friends for your book. They know me as well as anyone. Then I will talk with you."

Luiz Orlando speaks about Medium João:
My name is Luiz, but I am known by João as *Dos Ocolus* (The one with glasses). I was born in Rio de Janeiro. About ten years ago, Medium João paid me a great favor without knowing it. My daughter, Deborah, met him in Rio, and then she came to the Casa for a consultation with the Entities. Upon hearing that I lived in Itapaçi, Medium João personally brought her to visit me. She lives in America now, but for some reason we are estranged. This is her decision. I miss her.

Medium João interjects:
But she will read this message and be in touch with you.

Luiz's eyes misted over as he continued:
That would be an answer to my prayers. You see—no wonder Medium João has such an extraordinary reputation in this region and all over Brazil. He is always caring for others. In this town alone, he helps thousands with his care packages, kindness, and generosity. For years, I heard about this extraordinary man who is loved for his altruism and charity. It is with great pride that I am not only his friend, but we also have a trusting relationship in his gold-mining project. João, you can always count on me to be your loyal and faithful friend.

Medium João introduces Vilmar:

I would like you to meet Vilmar. He is my great friend and partner in our mining ventures. He has known me for many years. He knew my parents. He has known me as a tailor, and he has also accompanied me on my mission, not only in Goiás, but in many other states in our country.

Vilmar speaks about Medium João:

I am a little younger than João. I was born in 1953, but I have known João all of my life. One never forgets their childhood memories. I witnessed the hardships he experienced as a young boy. Poverty forced him to abandon his studies. Sometimes, we worked together at hard physical labor. Medium João never shirked hard work. The early years were very tough. This is a small town and work was scarce, so he had to leave in search of employment. His search brought him out into the world. In Mato Grosso, at the age of sixteen, he found his true purpose: to serve God and humanity. He has followed this duty faithfully ever since. Eventually, he opened his own tailoring and laundry-cleaning business to sustain a living while devoting his life to service.

I went out into the world and became a salesman who peddles carpets and bed linen. It was a tough time, but the silver lining was that I would meet up with Medium João on my travels. I would search him out. I am also a Spiritualist and have utmost faith in his work. We have never lost our friendship. We are now partners in the mineral mining business. Through employment, we sustain many families in this region. Our mining business is a vehicle for Medium João to help others. We employ workers in the area and sustain ancillary industries, but the underlying goal is always to maintain the Casa and other charitable projects.

We are more than friends; we are brothers. In that fraternal sense, our bond is deeper than our familial brothers. I can tell you with utmost conviction that it is my destiny in this lifetime to support João's mission. I've been to Europe, America, and South Korea on mining business. The intention is always for the expansion and success of the mine to support his mission for humanity. It is difficult to express my relationship with João and my enormous respect for his work. This would be a book in itself. Sometimes João says he wishes he could just rest for a day, but he is not in charge of his life. He has completely surrendered to God's work. The Entities call upon him at all times of the day and night. He must always be ready to do spiritual work yet also maintain his personal and business activities.

All afternoon, Ana had been trying to coax her husband into brushing his hair, which was disheveled after his siesta. He ignored her pleas for grooming and continued to lie on the tile floor listening to the interviews. Suddenly he sat up, gave her an impish grin, and began to brush his hair with a flourish. As he burst out laughing, Karen captured the moment.

Then he gave us an interview, often appearing to incorporate as he spoke and removing his glasses at different times. Karen, who was videotaping the interviews, began to feel the presence of the Entities, and she had to stop to reposition herself on the tile floor while holding the camera steady. She had felt the strong energetic presence of the Entities throughout most of the day, but now it became even more profound.

Heather: Medium João, were you in Itapaçi or Mato Grosso when you began fully incorporating the Entities of Light?

Medium João: All my life I have been a devout follower of Saint Rita of Cascia. I grew up as a Catholic from the crib. A Spiritist needs to read and study a lot, and I was unable to fulfill my studies because my mission began very early. The first time I received full incorporation was in Campo Grande at the Spiritist Center of

Christ the Redeemer. Since then, I have been on this mission for over forty-eight years. As you know, I have worked in nearly every state in Brazil, including the capital, as well as many other countries throughout the world.

I do not preach a religion, nor do I teach a religion. My belief is Universal. I believe in the Creator. I believe in Our Lady. I believe in the Apostles and the true Masonic Lodge. How can I even say that I am a Spiritist when I have met Chico Xavier, whom I call the *Pope of Spiritism*?[1] How can I compare myself to him? I was given the great honor of carrying Chico Xavier's body to his gravesite. I know that God is going to help me, and in this town of Itapaçi where we are all together today, my body will rest. That will be in your hands, for I know that I will eventually leave this plane. Like all good practicing Spiritists, I wish to join a phalange in the spiritual realm and practice charity and relieve human suffering. However, my body will be buried in Itapaçi alongside my mother, my brothers, and my father.

Heather: Please tell us what it was like visiting Greece and walking in the footsteps of the Apostle Paul. Was it a profound experience for you?

Medium João: I am glad you asked me. I believe the roots of many religions stem from Greece. The Spiritists and people of other religions—the Evangelists, Kardecists, and Catholics—also believe this. I was very well received by the good people of Greece. They took me to the spot where there is a plaque in honor of Apostle Paul. Ana is going to show you this photograph. I sat at that very spot and gave a message to those gathered with me. The message was not given by me, but by the "Men of Law," who are the Compassionate Spirits of faith [the Entities]. I have no knowledge. I do

1. Chico Xavier and Spiritism are discussed in later chapters.

not know anything. I cannot even write my own checks. I became lost and Ana found me in a church in the presence of priests as I was confessing.

Ana: Yes, it is true. Also the Orthodox bishop who accompanied the work and stood beside you every day wept in gratitude for all the healing he had received.

Medium João: I will return to Greece one day. It is good that my great friend Vilmar is here, because I have not told him about my honor—which God gave me—to be in the area where the Olympic Games were to be held. Ana was with me. As I began the opening ceremony for the spiritual work, Dr. Augusto de Almeida incorporated in me and gave a special blessing for the Olympic Games, which were scheduled to open a few weeks later.

Heather: We were grateful for your presence in Washington at the onset of the war with Iraq. Even though your brother had died just two days previously, you put everything aside and offered spiritual assistance.[2]

Medium João: You were with me in Washington D.C. that day in March 2003, but I can tell this to Vilmar. Ana was also present. A couple came. The man was a retired marine and their daughter was in the military in Iraq. They brought their daughter's photograph and asked for protection for her. The Entity assured the father that she would be completely protected.

Heather: I remember well, Medium João. I translated for the couple. The Entity asked them to return the next day with an item of her

2. Medium João traveled to Washington D.C. on March 20, 2003. It was a small gathering of about 120 people, and he called it a "mission of peace."

clothing. They brought one of her shirts, and the Entity told me to be sure to bring it to Brazil. When I returned to Brazil, I took the box with all the names and photographs to the Entity, and the first thing he wanted from me was the young woman's shirt. He held it in his hands for a moment and then carefully placed it in his basket. He also wanted to know when the parents and their daughter would be coming to Abadiânia. It was reported to me by a member of the group that she returned safe from Iraq.

Medium João: I know I have God with me, and also the Compassionate Spirits. No one walks alone. Christ did not walk alone, for there were not only the Twelve Apostles, there were 120 who accompanied him. [Medium João removes his glasses and appears to incorporate.] Christ proved there were another 4,000 accompanying him at the time he distributed the bread and the fishes. All were the Apostles of Christ. The Helping Spirits never walk alone. It is a phalange, a group of Compassionate Spirits who work together from the spiritual realms. I believe in Jesus, and I believe in God, for he is my Father. All that I do, all of my work, is for the Father. The Father gives me everything I need. For this reason I am a happy man. The heart of God watches over me.

Heather: Many people ask me what they can do to help with tragic world events, such as the tsunamis, floods, and wars. The world seems to be going through a crisis. Would you please comment on what we can do to help from a spiritual perspective?

Medium João: It is good that you ask me this question. First of all, respect one another and love God above all else. Love resolves everything. Let us wait for Love and the Word of God.

Heather: Thank you for spending time with us, Medium João, and for your delicious food and your hospitality. Thank you also for this interview. We are deeply and profoundly grateful for everything you do for us and for all of humanity.

Medium João: You are always welcome here. Come back another time and visit the gold mine. Vilmar and Luiz have my permission to show you around the land. It is a like a ring, a circle. The success of each project upholds the success of the Casa. You have come to interview and film the medium, but you see I am also a simple family man, a farmer, and miner.[3]

Heather: We understand that you have suffered, Medium João. Your good friend and attorney, Edemar, who has known you for over thirty-five years, has confirmed that you have been arrested and persecuted, and faced great dangers. With all that you have gone through, how can you continue to have so much dedication, generosity, and good humor?

Medium João: I know what you are trying to say. There were times when I was arrested, but never for murder or robbery, or any other serious crime. [He removes his glasses and begins to weep.] I was arrested for relaying the Word of God. There are those who believe that I am on this mission to make money. If that were the case, I would not be able to continue. I would have stopped years ago. The Word of God has a beginning but no end. The Word of God is

3. Heather visited Medium João's mine in 2006. Larger, international mining companies with state-of-the-art equipment, high walls, and guards surround and dwarf the mine. Medium João's camp portrays a stark contrast to the larger ones that border his; the operation was primitive and rustic, reminiscent of the 1850s, and the bounty humble; his team of prospectors was thrilled just to discover one gold nugget. "Dr. Augusto told us that the Entities guided him to acquire the mineral rights, but he is tired now, and the mine takes up a lot of his time," said Medium João. Due to financial challenges, Medium João closed the mining projects in the fall of 2006.

very beautiful, and She is eternal. I still want, one day, to reach the tribunal of Christ, the very heart of God.

Heather: In Portuguese, the word *Entity* is feminine. So we always refer to the Entity as She. Here, Medium João is referring to the Word of God as *She*. His words are profound and poetic when spoken in Portuguese, and we offer them to you in Medium João's own language:

> Porque a palavra de Deus ela tem começo ela não tem fim. Ela é muito bonita. Ela é eterna. Eu ainda quero um dia chegar no tribunal de Christo no seio de Deus.

Interview with Medium João at Itapaçi, Goiás, Brazil, February 5, 2005

ANA, THE WIFE OF MEDIUM JOÃO

Faith moves mountains; faith is what heals us, and faith is what guides us.

—Ana Teixeira Lorenço

In this chapter, Heather interviews Ana Keyla Teixeira Lorenço, the wife of Medium João. Ana begins by explaining that her family brought her to the Casa at a very young age. Eventually, through the intervention and tutelage of the Entities, it became evident that she was predestined to become Medium João's wife at this stage of his life. Ana gives us a rare and unique look into the life of João, the man, and João, the medium. She also offers great insight into the activities at the Casa, spirituality, and mediumship.

Ana: I first came to the Casa de Dom Inácio at the age of twelve with my family. I was brought up as a Catholic and a Spiritist, but my family actually leaned more towards Spiritism. From my very first visit, the Entity had me accompany him while doing the physical surgeries. I carried the instrument trays or the cotton wool and water. As I watched the physical surgeries, I was afraid that something like that would happen to me, so I would often disappear at the time of the incorporation. I would go down to the waterfall or out into

21

the garden. The Entity would call for me, but I would be out of sight. I would come back after the physical surgeries were over and join the line to go in front of the Entity. The Entity would call my family to discuss my mother's healing. He also explained the process of preparing and deepening her mediumship and my own.

Heather: On your initial visit to the Casa, did you have a particular illness or problem?

Ana: We came to the Casa primarily for the experience. I did not knowingly have an illness, but my mother had a cyst on her uterus. She received invisible surgery and the cyst was removed—it disappeared. We came back for my mother's revision forty days later and followed the protocol required by the Entities. We returned to the Casa regularly. At first, our visits were once a year. Due to the great distance from our hometown of Uberaba, in the State of Minas Gerais, more frequent visits were not possible. Eventually, a friendship ensued. Well not quite a friendship, because our work and our connection was with the Entities and mediums of the Casa, who would explain to us the Casa protocols and help us evolve spiritually. We rarely saw Medium João.

When I reached my early twenties, the Entities would always ask my mother and me to go and see Medium João in his office after the session. They encouraged us to make a connection with him. I was always reticent. I didn't know why, but I felt a ... resistance is perhaps a better way of explaining my feelings at the time. But now I understand what that resistance was all about. When I finally met Medium João, I felt like I already knew him. We already had a deep family bond. João—I will refer to him as João because he is my husband—said that he had the same recognition. There was a connection from the first time we met. I continued to come to the Casa, a little more frequently as the years wore on, but I never sought to deepen our friendship. Then one day, the Entity clarified many things for me and my mother in a long conversation. It was a *remembering*, a recollection that cleared my confusion. This conversation took place five years ago, after many, many visits to the Casa. João and I were married a year later. After this conversation, I had an understanding through the Entities of the past lives I had experienced with João. I knew we had always had our bond and our commitment to service.

Heather: Do you think the Entities brought you to the Casa at such a young age to reconnect you with Medium João so you could help him at this stage of his life?

Ana: I really can't fully answer that question, but I believe that nothing is by chance and that everyone has a mission on Earth. I know I am carrying out my mission and following my spiritual guidance.

Heather: For several years, we noticed that Medium João seemed sad, but when he talks about you there are stars in his eyes and he is radiant.

Ana: Now he is transformed, right? He says that I am his wonderful *companheira* (companion).

Heather: Are the members of your family Spiritists?

Ana: Yes. They are partly Spiritists and partly Catholic. I have two sisters and one brother. I was born in Minas Gerais, the *traingulo Mineiro*, which is a triangle that includes Brasília, Uberaba, and Goiânia. This area is known to hold a high vibration of energy. It is a well developed region with rich pastures that produce some of the best beef and dairy cattle in the area. Uberaba is the town where Francisco Cândido Xavier chose to live—*Chico*, as Brazilians lovingly know him.

Heather: Did you know Chico?

Ana: Oh yes. I knew him and participated in his work at his House of Prayer. He was a truly extraordinary person. I think the whole world lost a person who was pure heart when he passed.

Heather: I experience unconditional love when I am with Medium João and the Entities. This is something I never experienced before coming to the Casa. Did you experience this kind of love around Chico Xavier?

Ana: Yes, absolutely. It was extraordinary to be in his presence. We attended Chico's Christmas ceremony for many years. On Christmas Day, he would distribute gifts of money and food to the many people who lined up. His staff selected people over the preceding months, according to their needs, hardship, and extreme poverty. Over Christmas and for the following three days, these people would line up and Chico would give them a big smile, gentle words, a warm handshake, and compassionate guidance. He distributed the gifts personally. You could see the people felt they were receiving everything from his simple gestures and his deep compassion, love, and kindness.

Heather: Did Medium João spend a lot of time with Chico Xavier? I once asked him if he thought of Chico as his mentor, and he replied, "His word was a command to me."

Ana: Oh yes. They were good friends. Twice I had the pleasure of going with João to visit Chico. One time, Chico was physically quite weak. This was about two months before he died. His son, Euripides, told us that Chico would be delighted to receive João. Chico always dressed immaculately and was embarrassed to be seen in bed looking so frail and gaunt. He insisted on wearing the signature cap that he always wore. Chico broke into a huge smile when

João came into the room. As João bent down to hug him, Chico whispered something in his ear. I did not hear what Chico said, but I am certain João received and understood the message that was passed to him. It was an emotional time for us.

The next time we came down together was for his funeral. Chico Xavier was the leader of Spiritism. The motive for our last trip was very sad, but the spiritual vibrations were extraordinarily potent.

Heather: I heard that Chico sent a message to Medium João, some thirty years ago, saying Abadiânia was the place where the Casa should be built. Can you tell us anything about this?

Ana: João can give the best answer to this question, but I believe this is true. When I visited Chico with João, I saw for myself the deep consideration, respect, and love that Chico held for João. I have seen both the original and the 1993 re-channeled messages, the latter a small psychographed note by Chico from the Entity Bezerra de Menezes, designating Abadiânia as the place where João's mission would evolve.

Chico's re-channeled message signed and blessed for this book by Dom Inácio.

I had the wonderful privilege, during one of our visits to Uberaba, to take Medium João to the Spiritist Center I went to when I was growing up. The president of the center was also an old friend of

João's. He told us that he would be delighted to have João stay and attend to the people at his center. Unfortunately, due to lack of time and our need to return to Abadiânia, we were unable to stay. But something amazing happened that day. The president of the center told João that his mother had passed and how deeply he regretted not having even one photograph of her. João, the medium, was able to materialize a photo of this man's mother. This I saw with my own eyes. You can also ask João about this story and get his confirmation.

Heather: I have seen materializations of crystals by the Entities and know of many reports of similar materializations of stones, photographs, and crystals. Does this happen frequently at the Casa?

Ana: I believe this does happen at the Casa. I have not actually experienced materializations other than the incident I just described, but I have heard many testimonies from other people. For us, as Spiritists, this is not a mystery. I believe in materialization just as I believe in incorporation and the transporting of souls who are lost. I embrace everything that the Spiritist Gospel talks about and reveals to us.

Heather: There are many visitors coming to Abadiânia from all over the world, and this little village is becoming overcrowded, perhaps overwhelmed. How can we retain harmony and balance?

Ana: I believe the foreigners coming to Abadiânia are very positive for the village. By the same token, there is the negative aspect. Many times the spiritual focus is put aside, and perhaps the agenda becomes more commercial or material. More and more Brazilians come to me and say, "The Casa seems to be filled with foreigners. Do I have to be a foreigner to come to the Casa?" I tell them, "No. Absolutely not. This is João's home." João has had many invitations to live elsewhere in the world but he would never accept. His home, his true home, is here in Abadiânia, in Brazil.

The foreigners who come here have a different mentality from the Brazilians. Many of them are like St. Thomas, the doubter. They need to see to believe, and so they question more. They research more, they watch the surgeries, and they feel the energy. This intensified research is very good for the Casa because it validates the work. It serves to clarify doubts about the spiritual work performed at the Casa and even Medium João's management, conduct, and total dedication and commitment to service.

Heather: Many visitors do not completely follow the protocols required by the Entities. Sometimes, they do not honor and respect the ways of the Casa. We understand the requirements are given to us for our safety and for the healing to be more effective. My concern is that Abadiânia may become a spiritual "hangout" or that the Entities or Medium João may tire of the chaos that might evolve.

Ana: In the words of Medium João, "God is the one who cures— I do not cure anybody" (Quem cura é Deus eu não curo ninguem). We must always come with an open heart, because we are always in search of something. We come here because we are looking for a cure, either spiritual or physical. In this way, if we are searching for a healing—even if we are skeptical—we must come with open hearts. If we come to the Casa with a willing heart we will be shown our doubts and what we are able to believe.

There are countless examples of people who arrive at the Casa filled with misgivings and are tested. They witness surgeries and people having spontaneous healings. They watch in disbelief and ask, "How can this be happening?" They see it before their eyes, and yet there is no explanation. Some people return to the Casa a second time with clearer hearts. They are now more open and willing to accept the experience without negative emotions. This, in itself, is a healing. They no longer feel overwhelmed with suspicion. They are now more receptive to their healing. A person who is full of doubts and negative thoughts is not ready to receive healing—be it mental, emotional, physical, or spiritual.

Sometimes people come to the Casa with someone else who is in a wheelchair, or a friend in need, but then they also receive a deep healing. Although they were unaware of their own infirmity, they received the healing they needed. This is possible because they came with a surrendered heart and with faith. Faith moves mountains. Faith heals and guides us.

Heather: Do you agree that making a pilgrimage to the Casa and leaving behind the material comforts of home and facing the unknown is part of the healing process? Is the willingness to experience the simplicity and beauty of this land necessary for those seeking a deeper healing?

Ana: I have accompanied João on several trips abroad, and I have observed that sometimes a person requires treatment of a deeper nature. The energy of the Casa de Dom Inácio, the current of the Casa, is required for that treatment. The concentration and focus of the energy here is different, more potent. Each person should continue the treatment they were given by the Entity, while also understanding that if the Entity asks them to return to the Casa in Abadiânia, it will be for a deeper and more profound treatment.

Heather: Please tell us about your experiences in Greece with Medium João.

Ana: João attended the people of Greece in 2004, and I had the opportunity to go with him. We received a very warm welcome. João attended thousands of people over three days. Many of them were coming before the Entities for the first time, to take photos, or to embrace him. Everyone thanked him profusely.

An Orthodox bishop who participated on the first day impressed me. At the end of the session, the Entity spoke to the bishop and told him that he would cure him. The bishop was astounded. He had told no one about his illness. The bishop became emotional and wept. He came back every day. He entered the center praying; he prayed throughout the day; and he left still in prayer. I saw how he cried. He was astonished and asked the translator, "How could someone who comes from the other side (from spirit), whom I have never seen— I don't even know his name—point out the exact location of my illness?" The bishop stayed the entire three days, and on the last day he took off a medallion from around his neck and gave it to João.

Heather: Medium João told me that when he was in Greece he visited the place where the Apostle Paul had once stood. Did you go there, too?

Ana: Yes. We went to Placa, to the commemorative inscription at the site where the Apostle Paul taught. This was very moving for João. Another thing that impressed me was that so many people wanted João to visit their homes. We went to the homes of some people who had visited the Casa. To our delight, we saw many items reflecting the Casa: paintings of Dr. Augusto, Dr. Valdivino, and Dr. Oswaldo Cruz, and crystals and photos. Here, on the other side of the world, were photos of João and of him incorporated. We were extremely touched by this, as well as by the hospitality we received.

Heather: My house is also filled with images and photos of the Entities and Medium João. The experience of visiting the Casa has transformed the lives of millions of people. I have never met anyone who said they were not affected in a profound way.

Ana: No one has ever told me their life changed for the worse after visiting the Casa. On the contrary, they say how their lives have changed for the better, and some have been deeply transformed. This is a source of much joy. The Casa is unique for those of us who have a foundation in Spiritism. I believe there are very few mediums in the world who are able to carry out the work that Medium João does. I use the term *work*, meaning the work the Entities perform through him, since it is not João who does the work. The Entities are able to work through João because of his willingness to receive, to be present—and because of his dedication to service. I can truly say, as his wife, it is no easy task to serve because there is no set day or time. His commitment is constant. Many times we make a date to see a friend or one of his children, but we have to cancel. Our plans change all the time in order to attend to people in need. I see this as 100 percent total dedication. I have to say, if I were in his place I do not think I could make this much of a commitment. He gets up every morning at 2:00 A.M. to help people. As you know from being on trips with us, he sleeps very little.

Heather: Does he incorporate or work through prayer and meditation at night?

Ana: Each case is unique. Sometimes a person is in need of spiritual help, and through their prayers and thought they ask the Entities and Medium João for help. You can be sure that even if the person is on the other side of the world, they will receive energy transmitted through Medium João's focus and prayer, and their suffering will be alleviated. The Entities always respond.

Heather: You always seem serene and good-natured. Yet, this cannot be an easy life for you.

Ana: It is a little complicated at times for us. For example, most people have scheduled work hours and a time when they can be expected to come home. We cannot make firm plans. João often leaves the house at 3:00 or 4:00 A.M. or he comes home very late. We may make plans to have a quiet weekend or dinner with friends, and the next minute we are in São Paulo or some other city where João is called to work unexpectedly. His schedule is commanded from the highest spiritual levels. I always keep a bag packed so I can leave immediately.

Heather: You seem wise beyond your years.

Ana: The Entities have told me that I am a mature soul of many incarnations, but I do not really experience this. Yet, I know I am protected and guided by the Entities, and I am grateful to God.

Heather: Is it best to do spiritual work at 2:00 A.M.?

Ana: I think we should do our part at any time. Every time we pray, we bring spiritual benefit to ourselves and others. If we are able to join in prayer at a time when we know many others are also devoted to prayer, we can create a stronger current of energy. However, I have heard the Entities say to certain people, "Do your work at 2:00 A.M." Who am I to say when it is best to work? I think each person has free will and their own guidance. If you feel drawn to pray at a certain time, then simply open your heart to God at that time. When you go to bed, ask the Entities to bless you while you sleep through the night, and do your work at another time. I believe any time you set aside for meditation and prayer is beneficial.

Heather: Medium João told us in his interview about his visit to Washington D.C. in March 2003, one week after the war with Iraq was declared. We received his incredible invocation for world peace.

Ana: I thought it was providential that the visit took place at that location. The energy and focus of the people was very beautiful.

They showed their pristine intention for peace and healing for the planet. Their desire for a world without war was very powerful. The Entities brought through a very potent healing, as we all witnessed. We were grateful for the opportunity to work together for world peace, and, of course, many received spiritual and physical healing as well.

Heather: What do you and Medium João do for relaxation?

Ana: We love to cook simple food made with much love. Sometimes we invite close friends to share the evening with us. João loves to spend time on his farms, and he devotes a great deal of attention to them. He relies on the income from the farms and his mineral mines to run the Casa. It's important to remember that he supports other spiritual centers and soup kitchens in the country. There are many expenses. Over thirty full-time staff are employed at the Casa in Abadiânia alone. The expenses are vast. Not only the normal expenses, such as electricity, but he also offers free soup at the Casa and the soup kitchen at the other end of town. The staff and many volunteers receive a full lunch every day. Donations and contributions do not cover these expenses, so he takes from his personal income to support his commitments. He works hard in his mining, farming, and business projects in order to sustain the Casa. He also helps countless people with their college and university education. João sponsors many, but he never talks about it. I think he is such an immaculate example of generosity and charity. He gives to those in need without strings and with such grace. When a person needs a wheelchair, a temporary home, or education, he answers the call. Medium João has built a Casa in the south of Brazil that helps rehabilitate those afflicted with addictions.

Heather: What advice would you give someone coming to the Casa for the first time?

Ana: When you enter the Casa for the first time, actually every time, pray to the Divine Source—whatever that is for you—for the grace to achieve the healing you are seeking, be it spiritual, physical, or emotional, or the healing of a relationship. Come with an open heart for all that you seek and with faith you will be healed. I have received so much at the Casa, and I believe it is because of my deep faith. Not only was my mother healed, but also my brother received a nonphysical operation. At that time, he did not comprehend the nature of the healing. He felt that he was healthy. But now he has complete understanding of what transpired.

I have received not only physical healings but also resolution of day-to-day problems in the mundane world. If we come with faith and willingness, we receive. And, most importantly, it is through prayer and focused concentration in the current rooms that the Entities attend to us. It is not necessary to go to the Entities with every request for assistance and clarification. The Entities can see what we need. They might ask us to write down our questions. Sometimes our time in front of the Entity is limited, but we can give the Entity a more detailed written request.

Heather: I believe that if we approach the Entity with the belief "Father, I have faith in you to help me," the Entities read our vibrations, thoughts, and real desires. Do you agree?

Ana: I believe the soul is reached through the eyes. I think the Entities see us as if we are transparent; it's like looking through clear glass. I believe everything that is unwell in us originates on the spiritual level. The Entities see into the origin of the issue. For example, if a person has a bladder problem, the cause might be spiritual or emotional. The physical bladder will be cured when these issues are corrected. The physical is always the last to be healed. Also, perhaps the problem manifests in the bladder but originates in another organ. When that organ becomes healthy, the bladder will heal.

Heather: Is it true that when we approach the Entity with faith, saying, "I have faith, Father, that you know what is needed for my deepest healing," we give the Entities the freedom and permission to work on the root cause of our problems and bypass our limitations?

Ana: We have free will choice. The Entities do not do the work without permission. It depends on what the person wants. You must have witnessed times when the Entity tells a person that he needs work. The Entity asks if the person wishes the treatment to be carried out. Will they return the required number of times? If the person refuses, they have made a choice and the Entity will not insist. Perhaps sometime later the person may return and say they are ready to be cured. The Entities will help, of course, but perhaps too much time has passed and the situation is now more complicated. It all revolves around the merit, faith, and free will choice of the individual.

Heather: I understand. You mean the willingness to stand before the Entities and give God permission to heal you sets the stage for greater healing.

Ana: I understand this to be true. We are all related, all brothers and sisters. The Entities do not distinguish one person as being more worthy than another. They love us all equally. Sometimes the Entity spends a long time talking to one person, but you can be sure he is attending to everyone at the same time. There is no favoritism. Sometimes people feel it was so fast for them in the line. They say, "But when so-and-so passed through the line they spent a long time talking with the Entity." Right there is a spiritual slip, because that person is feeling jealous. We need to love each other without disparity. We must strive to be immaculate in our thinking. When we have these negative thoughts, when we focus on the person who is spending more time with the Entity, when we feel envy and resentment, then we are slipping. We are always giving and receiving energy, and our thoughts can pollute the current. We may feel sad when we pass before the Entity and he seems to pay us no attention. We may be desperate for a gentle word of encouragement, but think of it as a good sign that today another person needs the attention more and you are fine. Being in the current is a great opportunity to give and receive God's grace. Every time I am told to go to the current, I give thanks for one more opportunity to be in this sacred space.

Heather: I believe that when we sit in the current it is best to open our hearts to be a channel of healing for ourselves and for all our brothers and sisters. In this way, we open up to the healing light for the highest good for all. Is this the idea?

Ana: Yes. No one is perfect. We are connected to the Divine when we are in the current. We are close to God and we can seek forgiveness for our faults. By faults, I mean offending others with our unconscious behavior; for example, an angry retort or an envious remark. We open our hearts and communicate with God and receive guidance when we are in the current. We receive the divine blessings from the phalange of light that is working for us. We can send the light to assist the Entities, visualize the rooms filled with light, and follow our intuition.

Heather: Ana, thank you for sharing your wisdom, and for your kindness, love, and compassion.

Ana: I also want to thank you, Heather, for your help, generosity, and devotion to the Casa.

Interview with Ana Teixeira Lorenço at Anápolis, Brazil, February 22, 2005

THE ROAD TO THE CASA

*Between the 15th and 20th parallels, where a lake has formed,
a great civilization will be born.*

—Dom Bosco

After landing in Brasília at one of the most charming airports in the world, the atmosphere of Brazil immediately begins to come alive. The open-air compound with ticket counters and food vendors is busy with people coming and going. Meeting the Brazilian people for the first time, you notice how strikingly beautiful and joyful they are. There is an ease about them. No matter what their hardships, they are usually happy.

The taxi drivers usually pick up and escort guests back to Abadiânia, about one and a half hours away. The fragrance of sweet grass blows through the open windows. Rolling, tumultuous cloud formations cascade with light and color that delights the senses. They seem close enough to reach up and touch.

Brasília is the capital of Brazil and was built according to the vision of Dom Bosco, an Italian priest born in 1815 and founder of the Silesian Order. Dom Bosco had a prophetic dream in 1833, about which he said, in part: "Between the 15th and 20th parallels

37

there is a long, wide depression in the vicinity of a lake. When they come to explore the riches buried in these mountains, here will rise a promised land of milk and honey of unconceivable wealth."

President Juscelino Kubitschek fulfilled his campaign promise to build the new capital following Dom Bosco's guidance. Built in the 1960s, the city is shaped like an airplane; the fuselage contains the ministries and government buildings, and the wing area contains the hotels, business district, and homes. The residences of Brazil's president and vice presidents are situated in the "cockpit." The city's original designer was the futuristic architect Oscar Niemeyer.

Abadiânia is situated approximately 115 kilometers (71 miles) south of Brasília. The average temperature is 20.5°C (69°F). The hottest month is December, with an average high of 29°C (85°F); the coolest month is July, with an average low of 13°C (55°F). Abadiânia has a population of 12,750; this figure includes the surrounding municipality. The altitude is 1,052 meters above sea level (3,451 feet).

The road to Abadiânia passes through virgin forest, rolling hills, and fertile pastureland studded with herds of white Brahmin cattle. Before long, the small town of Abadiânia appears. Although it was once a quiet, dusty village, the infusion of foreigners has brought growth to the community. Still, the shops are small adobe houses built with local bricks. More and more *pousadas* (small hotels) have sprung up along the road to house the thousands of people who come to see John of God: from three hundred to two thousand each day.

Dressed completely in white, guests walk down the main street for their first morning current session. The Entities of light who work through John of God prefer visitors to wear white because it makes their auric energy fields more visible. People in wheelchairs, the old and young, the blind, and those with all manner of ailments approach the Casa de Dom Inácio de Loyola on a quest for healing. New gates to the Casa have recently been built, and the energy of healing can be felt as soon you walk through them. Inexplicable but palpable, the Entities are already at work; your inner landscape begins to change. One can breathe easier in this atmosphere of spiritual love, let go of burden, and attend to prayer.

Straight ahead from the gates is the crystal shop, a tiny structure that distributes tickets for entry into the "current rooms" and passage before the Entity. The shop has books, rosaries, crystals, and, most importantly, water blessed by the Entities for sale. Walking toward the main hall, where everyone gathers for the current room sessions, a snack bar offers local food and delicacies, juices, and delicious fresh coconut water. Across the way, there is a room filled with paraphernalia that is no longer needed—canes, wheelchairs, and eyeglasses are piled at random.

The main hall has comfortable chairs and benches, where guests wait for the sessions to begin on a small stage at the front of the room. There are pictures of the Entities, Jesus, and spirit photos hanging on the walls around us. A small television shows videos of John of God performing surgeries. The surgery room, the Entity's current rooms, and an infirmary with twelve beds are located behind the doors at the front of the hall. Visitors spend much of their time in prayer and meditation in these areas. Volunteers in the infirmary attend to people who are recovering from physical surgery until they are able to return to their pousadas for complete rest. The Casa gardens are resplendent with flowers and mango and avocado trees. The meditation deck looks out over a magnificent landscape with spectacular crimson sunsets in the evenings. The valley below spreads for miles to a plateau in the distance and is forested with flowering trees and a red-clay dirt road—so typical of Brazil—which leads to the sacred waterfall, hidden from view. The building that houses the crystal treatment rooms is located to the right, next to the gardens.

The Casa is designed to accommodate hundreds of visitors each day. Across from the garden is the kitchen, where a spiritual soup is prepared on Wednesday, Thursday, and Friday for guests of the Casa. This compound is a sacred space, and everyone who comes here is asked to show kindness and respect to all brothers and sisters while at the Casa. *Everyone's* healing is prayed for, because when one person is healed, all are healed. A life of balance and harmony—this is the peace and tranquillity of the Casa.

Guests take walks in the valley during the quiet of the early morning mist. Tuning in to the rhythm of this beautiful land, we are often gifted with glimpses of blue and yellow or red macaws, parrots, hummingbirds, hawks, toucans, woodpeckers, and secretary birds. Owls are also a common sight in Abadiânia.

The Entities, recognizing the ongoing influx of people, began expanding the infrastructure of the Casa to accommodate everyone. A new extension to the Entity's current room was completed in 2004, and ventilation was added in all of the current rooms. Many of the tour guides and grateful visitors donate time and finances for improvement projects. Donations are also requested to help with the expansion of the Casa.

FILHOS OF THE CASA

Many wonderful people work and volunteer at the Casa to help maintain Medium João's mission. A few of their stories are included in the following pages, but there are many filhos who devote their lives to support the Casa, and they are important to the success of this work. Unfortunately, we can only include a small selection due to space limitations, but many more stories of miraculous healings can be found in Chapter 10.

▲

A CHANCE MEETING
Sebastião da Silva Lima

Sebastião (Sebastian) was born in 1952, in Olhos De'Agua, Goiás, Brazil. He is the official Casa Secretary. Sebastian greets every visitor on Casa days, every Wednesday, Thursday, and Friday, whether Medium João is at the Casa or traveling. He is a deeply evolved, astute medium, who has been in service to the Casa for over thirty years. Also fondly known as Tião, he is a trained nurse and school-teacher, and he spent eight years in the seminary. Sebastian begins the Casa sessions with welcoming prayers.

Sebastian first met Medium João by chance. He was smitten by a pretty young lady, who was a "wailer." In those days, there were people who were paid to wail and cry at wakes. He went to a center where she worked, and there he encountered the Entities for the first time. He was told to meet with Medium João afterward.

Sebastian speaks about Medium João:
It was extremely confusing. His eyes would change color: brown, green, and then the deepest blue. When I first met João, he told me he had been waiting for me for a long time. We became friends, and I have been with him ever since. His mother, Dona Iuca, was the dearest woman. She treated me like her son and asked me to always stay close to João. I have seen so many wonderful healings, from AIDS to restoring sight to the blind. One time, the Entity told three men, "Those who do not have faith cut my skin." He showed them where to cut Medium João's chest area. When he passed his hand over the bleeding wound, it healed and knitted together before our eyes. Sometimes the Entity would look at a person and then tell them to lift their shirt. There would be a cut where surgery had been performed without them ever being touched. He would often pass his hands over wounds and they would heal instantly.

When Medium João had a stroke and was left with semi-paralysis down one side, the Entities performed surgery on him and he came back to normal, as you see him now. When this site was chosen for the Casa, Dom Inácio incorporated and marked the site where the wall of the main hall and triangle is now. One time, we were questioned at the police station—in those days this was a frequent occurrence, although now he is allowed to work without difficulties. The Entity incorporated and told the sheriff that he knew his daughter had a heart condition and was due for surgery at the hospital. The sixteen-year-old was brought before him, and he laid a kitchen knife just above her heart, flat without cutting. That night she was in much pain and was taken to the hospital. X-rays were taken and internal stitches were visible around the area of pain. Eight days later, her parents brought her for revision. The sheriff's daughter was healed and never needed further surgery. I believe we were detained for questioning that day in order to help this young woman. So here I am, and I will continue to serve at Medium João's side for as long as I am needed.

I have told the following rosary story many times. I was with Medium João and two others from the Casa in São Paulo. As we were preparing to return home, a man came up to me and handed me four, small, wooden rosaries. I looked at them and then looked up to thank the man, but he had completely disappeared. We were perplexed, but we were used to strange things happening around Medium João. We never knew what to expect. I put one rosary in João's shirt pocket and one in each of the other men's pockets. We chatted and then parted. They were returning by bus, and we were catching a plane. A pilot who was a frequent visitor to the Casa had given us free tickets. Medium João fell asleep while waiting for our flight to be called, and I simply could not rouse him. We missed our flight. I was upset, but Medium João was very excited. He said the beautiful woman had come to him again. It was such a vivid dream that he did not want to wake from it. He meant Santa Rita. We caught the next flight departure.

About halfway through the flight, we were called up to the airplane cockpit. This was a fairly normal occurrence because Medium João is well known. We were told not to worry, but there had been an accident when the flight we had missed landed, and somehow we were still on the passenger list. They wanted to radio our names to the airport in Goiânia so our families could be reassured that we were unharmed. The television news was expected to report the accident, and there was much chaos at the airport. We were very grateful that we had missed the earlier flight.

I reached into my pocket and there was the rosary I had been given, but it was broken. I showed it to João, and he reached into his pocket and pulled out a similarly splintered rosary. I called my friends the next day. When they checked their pockets, their two rosaries were also shattered. I believe we had protective and powerful energy that day.

▲

A SENSE OF URGENCY
Martin Mosqueira

Martin is a translator and one of Medium João's main assistants. He is good-natured, patient, compassionate, and devoted to Medium João's mission. He is responsible for building improvements and projects at the Casa, including a new soup kitchen in Abadiânia. In addition to their responsibilities at the Casa, Martin and his wife, Fernanda, run two pousadas: *Namaste* and *Irmão Sol Irma Lua*. Many times the Entity has told Martin, "Don't worry. You will never be in a wheelchair."

Martin explains how the Entities reassured him:
I first came to the Casa from Argentina in 1993. My mother brought me here. I took my mother to see a specialist for her chronic back pain. The doctor ran all sorts of tests, a complete checkup, and then he told her to go to Brazil and see John of God.

Later, we were driving through Buenos Aires—you know it is a huge sprawling city—on our way home to La Plata. After driving for about two hours, we stopped at the outskirts of town to gas up and have a meal. It was a simple eatery at a truck stop. We ordered our food and started talking with another customer. We chatted about many things, but then he told my mother she should go to Brazil and visit John of God because he could help her back condition. Well, that got our attention. It was no coincidence to be told twice to go to Brazil in less than two hours. Of course, we came here to Abadiânia. I immediately felt very comfortable. I felt at home. I met Fernanda in Abadiânia and we got married. Soon, we opened our first pousada. My mother has a house here now, too, and she spends a lot of time working in the current room in the Casa. There are so many stories of healing I could tell, but here is the one about my back:

It was in April of 2000, when my son was only a month old. I was playing with my stepson and was throwing a toy airplane back and forth. Then it flew up on my neighbor's roof. She was away and her house was empty, so I climbed up onto the roof to bring it back. I tried to walk very carefully over the tiles, but suddenly my foot broke a roof tile and I fell through the roof and landed on the tile floor below. Wham! It was hard. I must have broken my fall with my left hand because I felt a searing pain in my hand. I looked at my arm and saw the bone sticking up at a 75-degree angle to my hand. The skin was not broken, but the arm definitely was. I was lying on my back. I got up slowly; my back was only a little painful, but my hand needed immediate attention. We went to the Orthopedic Hospital in Anápolis. The doctor wanted to operate and put in screws and a metal plate. I refused to have all that and settled for a cast to set the bone. The next day, Friday, I went before the Entity. He seemed very "ho hum" about it. He just shrugged and told me to sit in the current.

The pain really started to get bad over the weekend. My hand became very swollen and was straining against the cast. The pain was intense and my hand throbbed constantly. I went to the Entity again on Wednesday, showed him my swollen hand, and told him about the pain. He said, "You should be happy. You would have been in a wheelchair." He told me to sit in the current and he would help. The pain intensified as I sat there. I felt a really hot spot, as if someone was holding a lighted cigarette onto my thumb just below the nail. The pain in that spot was excruciating. I peeked to see if someone was holding a cigarette to me. At the end of the session, the pain and hot spot immediately stopped, but when I looked at my thumb there was a small cut and a black and blue circle where I had felt the burning sensation. Look, here is the scar.

(The Entity) Dr. Augusto told me he had done *trabalho*, a term the Entities use to describe their spirtitual work. Two months later, Dr. Augusto called for Antão and asked him to take my cast off. We went outside and Antão started sawing with a wood saw. It was a little scary, but he removed the cast perfectly. My hand and arm were heavy, limp, and unresponsive. The Entity told me not to worry; with time and exercise it would get strong again. It's just perfect now. No screws or metal plates were needed.

On September 27 of that year, the Entity told us not to eat red meat until further notice and that in ninety days he would have a surprise for me. I marked the calendar. In December, I drove my family down to Argentina, taking it slowly, visiting Fernanda's family on the way. On December 17, at my family's home in La Plata, I suddenly had severe back pain that became progressively worse. By Christmas Eve, the pain was so bad I was doubled over and walking stooped, almost at a right angle to my waist. My family took me to a doctor, who prescribed strong antiinflammatory pills and told me I needed a CAT scan. The situation became much worse, and on Christmas day a friend who owned a clinic opened her office and ran a CAT scan for me. Two days after Christmas, I met with a renowned specialist in La Plata. He looked at the scan and told me in no uncertain terms that I must have surgery immediately. The disks on L5 and SI were badly herniated, over two centimeters. When I bent to pick a paper off the floor, he was horrified and told me I must not bend over. Even just walking along the street, I could collapse and end up paralyzed and in a wheelchair. There was a real sense of urgency.

The date was December 27—exactly ninety days after the Entity had said he would have a surprise for me. I was shattered. My family wanted me to have the surgery immediately, but I felt torn. I knew in my heart the Entities could heal this, but how was I going to get back to Abadiânia? The next few days were extremely stressful. My family was exasperated with me for delaying the surgery, because the doctor had convinced them of my precarious condition.

I could not sleep. Every position, standing or lying, was agony. The pain was excruciating and never let up. The surgeon took me off muscle relaxants and gave me morphine. He said that relaxing the muscles could provoke further trauma and the herniated disk might pop completely. This would mean paralysis for sure. The surgeon had seen many cases similar to mine but none as severe. He had developed a special surgical procedure to correct this form of disk condition, and there was a reported 80 percent success rate. He had helped many long-distance truck and bus drivers who suffered from the same problem. The prognosis was dismal without treatment.

I called Medium João, who said the Entities were looking into the situation. He instructed Fernanda to dress us both in white clothes and to work on me at 2:00 A.M. with prayer and hands-on healing. The Entities told her they would help me. When I called again, Medium João told me to come back to the Casa by whatever means: bus, plane, truck, or horse and cart. The choice was mine, but he would assume complete responsibility. He said the Entities had promised they would handle my situation. To my family's horror, I decided to drive. My sister came with us and drove half of the three thousand kilometers. It was like deciding to jump blindfold into a deep pool, not knowing for sure if the pool contained water. But I believe in the Entities, and if people come from all over the world to be treated by them, then I must also trust and have faith. If the Entities had told me to stay in Argentina and have surgery, I would have done so.

We arrived in Abadiânia on a Friday night, but I had to wait until Wednesday to consult with the Entities. The doctor had given me morphine, but it hardly helped. On Wednesday, the Entity told me to come back for an operation at 2:00 P.M. When the time came, I lay on the *maca* bed. This is a massage table in the surgery room that is used for deep healing. I closed my eyes and adjusted my body to find a comfortable position. It seemed like only a second, but when I opened my eyes I saw people filing past. I waited to hear Sebastian's words preparing us for surgery, but instead someone came to get me up. It was the end of the session. I had experienced a complete lapse in time. The entire session, over an hour and a half, had passed in the blink of an eye. I was exhausted and went home to rest, feeling it was important to take the Entities' directions seriously. After eight days, I slowly began to get stronger.

One day, the Entity (Dr. Augusto) lifted my shirt and ran his hand, or perhaps a scalpel, along my lower spine. Another time, when he slapped my lower back, I felt a jog like everything was going into alignment. The pain began to decrease slowly over the next two months, until one day I woke up and there was no pain. As you know, my back is now straight, strong, and fully recovered.

Surrogate surgery is performed for a person who is unable to be at the Casa. With the Entities' permission and direction, the surrogate goes into the surgery room on the appointed day and focuses on the friend in need, who is at home. However, the person receiving the healing follows the diet. The Entity sent a friend to the waterfall to be the surrogate for the work they wanted done for me at the waterfall. In Martin's case his friend represented him at the waterfall.

▲

LUCAS WANTS A BROTHER
Sandro Teixeira de Faria

Sandro is one of Medium João's sons. He is a law school graduate and has worked at the Casa for many years. Sandro oversees the production of the DVDs and videos and handles other computer- and business-related matters. He speaks often about being the son of one of the most powerful healers in the world. It has not been easy for him to live in his father's shadow, but he deeply loves João and admires him greatly. Sandro has an engaging manner and a brilliant smile.

Sandro's son, Lucas, brings him great joy. Over the last couple of years, Lucas has gone to the Entity (Dr. Augusto) numerous times and said, "Vovo (Grandpa), I want a brother. I am tired of being an only child."

"Now we have another miracle on the way." Sandro lights up as he offers the thrilling news. "My wife's tubes are tied, and I had a very bad auto accident some years ago that culminated in a vasectomy. We thought we could not have children, but now my wife has given birth to our second son, a gift from the Entities. Perhaps also thanks to the persistence of our son Lucas."

▲

DOM INÁCIO BRINGS A DOCTOR THROUGH THE BARDO
Dr. Roger

Dr. Roger Queiroz was a psychiatrist at a prominent hospital in Brasília, Brazil. He was skeptical concerning spiritual matters and came to the Casa only to bring his mother and wife. He refused all offers of assistance from the Entities for himself. He enjoyed his visits to the Casa because the people were kind and friendly, yet he ridiculed the treatments and surgeries. High blood pressure, lack of exercise, and a rich diet had provoked heart disease at the age of 49.

The Entity offered to perform surgery on him, telling him he would be cured, but Dr. Roger adamantly refused.

His condition worsened until eventually he required surgery. Dr. Roger went into the hospital to be operated on by his colleagues. While waiting to be taken for surgery, he felt a presence, a spirit that seemed helpful. Nonsense, he thought. *I must be unnerved by the prospect of surgery and my family's constant chatter about spirits.* Moments later, he suffered a massive heart attack and was rushed to the ICU, but it was too late. Dr. Roger died on the table. The surgeon told Dr. Roger's wife, Marilene, who phoned the Casa immediately and asked Sebastian to please go to the Entity with the information. Sebastian took the telephone to the Entity, who said the body must not be removed from the ICU until after 3:00 P.M. She was to remain with the body. Dr. Roger was receiving help and his body must *not* be moved.

The death certificate cited the time of death as 10:15 A.M. It is unheard of in Brazil to leave a body for so long in the ICU after death. Burial usually takes place within twenty-four hours. However, since he had been a colleague and worked in the hospital, the surgeon took pity on the widow and left an order that the body should not be removed until his return at 3:00 P.M. A nurse was to remain with the body.

Dr. Roger, meanwhile, felt himself soaring over the Casa. He was taken deep into the Earth, where he saw the crystal quartz beds and the stream that flows under the Casa. He reports that he refreshed himself in this exquisite flow of water. At the same moment, while his body lay in the ICU, the nurse reported that, inexplicably, water had drenched his torso and spilled onto the floor.

Next, his journey took him to a place of extraordinary suffering, an area of darkness where people roamed aimlessly, lost, troubled, and lonely. When he recounts this part of his story, he invariably struggles with tears. It is a vivid and horrific memory.

Out of the mists, he was approached by a priest (Dom Inácio). At this point, Dr. Roger became confused. He wondered, *Why would a priest seek me out? I am a nonbeliever and have frequently ridiculed the "men of the cloth" and the church.*

The Entity (Dom Inácio) announced himself and embraced Dr. Roger. Then he took him to a place of exquisite beauty. Dr. Roger marveled at the splendor of his surroundings—the likes of which he had never seen before. It surpassed his imagination. He asked Dom Inácio why they were together, and he explained that he had often accompanied his wife to the Casa, but he had no belief in the work. Dom Inácio counseled Dr. Roger, explaining that he was no longer in his body. He continued with profound teachings and told Dr. Roger that he had much work to do and would help many people. Dr. Roger was reminded of his free will and that ultimately the decision would be his. When he agreed to carry out the spiritual work suggested by Dom Inácio, he was told he would be returned to his body to resume his life on Earth.

Dr. Roger opened his eyes and asked for water a little before 3:00 P.M. The nurse ran out of the room in shock. Dr. Roger was impressed with her quick reaction but soon became anxious because the water was not forthcoming. Two nurses peered in through the slightly opened door, but they did not enter. Finally, a doctor arrived and thoroughly examined him. He was incredulous, because Dr. Roger was alive and appeared to have no brain damage. Over the next two days, the doctors conducted a battery of tests, but no explanation was found and Dr. Roger was discharged from the hospital. Following the directives of Dom Inácio, he went without delay to the Casa with his wife. As he crossed the main hall on his way to the current room, Medium João walked out of his office and embraced Dr. Roger, whispering in his ear: "Son, it was arduous, but you are home. Now there is work to be done." It was actually Dom Inácio, who incorporated into Medium João and had spoken those words.

Dr. Roger's life has changed completely. He travels at the invitation of spiritual organizations to tell his story. He is slim and healthy, and his life is one of service. He has helped many people who are depressed and on the brink of suicide.

One time, as he and Marilene were leaving Rio to return home to Brasília, he felt himself being "pulled back." He has learned to answer the call. They went to Copacabana and had lunch while they waited on the beach to see what would happen. He watched a woman who was jumping into the waves, submerging, and then being tossed around violently by the current and dumped back on the sand. The current is dangerous at this area of the beach and a strong wind was up. The woman repeated this process several times, becoming visibly weaker in her efforts. Dr. Roger was perplexed and walked over to her. He saw that she was elderly. "Listen, the tide is dangerous. You could drown," he said. She was angry and told him to leave her alone, because she was trying to do just that—drown herself. She felt she had no reason to live.

Dr. Roger stayed with her and related his story to her. He, too, had thought his life was empty and shallow, but now he cherished every moment with gratitude. The woman broke down and asked Dr. Roger and his wife to take her home. She lived in a huge apartment a block from the beach. She owned most of the building. She admitted to feeling materially rich but spiritually destitute. She is a different woman now and has embraced life with a passion. She and Dr. Roger have become good friends.

Dr. Roger has many other such stories to tell about his mission. He is a happy man. He says he will leave this world when Dom Inácio calls for him. It is not yet his time, but he will be ready and has no fear. Dr. Roger has received a spiritual awakening and understands his mission.

Sebastian reminds us that it is Dr. Roger's wife who must be honored, because it was her faith that prompted her to call the Casa for help. It took immense courage and conviction for a woman in grief to challenge the medical authorities and convince them not to transfer her husband's body to the morgue.

▲

DEBUNKING A CHARLATAN
Edemar Goncalves Rocha

In 1973, Edemar visited his friend Niltacio, who was sick. His wife, Nati, was upset because a healer had come to their house saying that if they would lend him their jewelry and watches, he would return them energized and Niltacio would be healed. Unfortunately, he was a charlatan who stole their possessions.

Edemar was upset by these circumstances and, being a lawyer, he felt it was his duty to find the thief and recover their stolen belongings. Later that afternoon, he picked up his wife at the school where she worked, as usual. She was excited because a great healer, John of God, was visiting a friend and co-worker. This healer, she said, was like the famous trance medium Zé Arrigo, who incorporated Dr. Fritz (the spirit of a famous German surgeon). She wanted Edemar to go with her immediately and meet him.

Edemar tells the story:

Believing this man must be the same impostor who had robbed my friends, I was eager to get there as soon as possible to expose him and have him arrested. Knowing me to be a skeptic, my wife was surprised at my willingness to accompany her, but I kept my true reasons to myself.

Upon arriving at Maria's house, I walked up to the medium and asked if I could watch closely. Medium João replied, "Of course; this is for everybody to see." Then he incorporated and invited me to stand beside him. He asked a woman to sit on a small stool in front of him, and he operated on her by first wiping her eye with cotton wool dipped in holy water. Then he scraped her eye with a paring knife. It was a common kitchen knife with a serrated blade. Her face was serene; she never flinched during the entire operation. I watched very carefully from less than a foot away. Later, she said she felt no pain. I was astonished. It was definitely not staged, as I had expected.

After the surgery, I asked the Entity, "Will you tell me what I need?" The Entity said it was surgery in my left eye. Again, I was astounded. Just a few weeks before, I had gone to the optometrist with an acute eye irritation. The doctor had explained that the tear duct was obstructed and I would need surgery. Nobody knew that I had been to an eye doctor, not even my wife. This was confirmation of the truth manifesting before me. The Entity invited me to sit down. I was terrified and began to perspire profusely, believing my eye would be scraped. The Entity asked me to face the crowd. I wanted to bolt from there; I trembled with fear. But, I reasoned, I am well known in the area. I have a good reputation as a successful and somewhat tough and uncompromising lawyer. I took on the most difficult cases and had a good success record, not only in my state, but in many other states where I worked. How would it look if I became a coward and ran out after this woman had allowed her eye to be scraped? My reputation would be shattered. The crowd would ridicule me and I would lose my clients. So, I remained, albeit reluctantly.

The Entity gently swabbed out my eye with holy water and scraped it with a swab, not the knife. I felt absolutely no pain. My eye was healed immediately, and I never required surgery on the tear duct. Then I asked the Entity to help my hearing problem. I was a pilot and needed acute hearing for my license exam. The Entity said, "I could heal this ear now, but it is a payment from a past life. If I heal you of this problem now, another situation will appear on your body, possibly even worse, because you are paying off a debt from a past life. I can't heal this now because you are not spiritually ripe. You need to do service and work this off spiritually. Then I can take care of your problem."

Over the years, my ear problem has not gotten worse. I went to a surgeon who said he could do an operation, but at great risk. I chose to heed the advice of the Entity and live with my hearing condition. We never caught the thief, but I met the true healer, João de Deus. I also found in him a wonderful friend.

Edemar continues:

This is not fiction. I am only satisfied when I can include all the details and the absolute truth. I hope you will bear with me. The first time I came to Abadiânia, the Casa was on the other side of the highway in a tiny house. I was living in Colinas at that time, but I went to Coneicão da Araguaia in the State of Para on business and to visit my cousin. As I approached my cousin, he was saying to friends that he wanted to find the healer who performed miracles. I said, "I know him. His name is *João de Deus.* He is my friend, but I have lost contact with him." Alberto's mother, my aunt, was desperately ill and unable to travel. He asked me to find João and bring him back to Para to heal her. I had heard that Medium João was working in Abadiânia, and so I traveled nonstop throughout the night to find him.

When I arrived at the rustic shack where Medium João performed his work, there were already one hundred cars there. As João's car approached, I was concerned. Would he recognize me in the crowd? It had been many years since we had seen each other. Immediately upon stepping out of the car, Medium João said, "How are you, Edemar?" He invited me to stay at his house in Anápolis. From there, he graciously returned the 2,000 kilometers (1240 miles) to Para with me and successfully treated my aunt. I believe this speaks volumes about the depth of his friendship, his commitment to his work, and his loving kindness.

On another occasion, Medium João was arrested in Arapoema, State of Tocantins. We had become good friends by that time. Occasionally, the Medium called on me for legal services. I went to the jail to bail him out. Over the years, disgruntled physicians and vengeful religious skeptics have sought to have him arrested. Although Medium João has suffered at the hands of the authorities, he feels he has a very blessed life and says he has never suffered. He never complains about these events. After being released, the mayor allowed Medium João to use the new school building for his work. I witnessed many wonderful healings at this school. Once, a woman was carried in completely incapacitated. She was paralyzed and was carried in using a deck chair. She was able to walk out of the school after her surgery. This is but one of hundreds of cures I have seen performed by the Entities with my own eyes.

Years later, Medium João came to Colinas where I lived. He was working and staying at the house of the mayor. I went to visit the Medium where he was working. The Entity who incorporated that day was Saint Ignatius de Loyola. I asked him, "Are you Saint Ignatius of Loyola?" He answered, "Dom Inácio is sufficient." (There are no saints in Spiritism because from the universal perspective everyone is equal.) Dom Inácio told me to accompany Medium João and a small group of people to a river on the outskirts of town. He said I should wear a white shirt and go with Medium João into the water. Dom Inácio instructed me to say the *Our Father* prayer in my mind as I stood in the river, and then call out the name "John the Baptist." The Entity told me, "You will see what happens."

When we arrived at the river, I did as instructed. I prayed and then called out "John the Baptist." Medium João immediately incorporated. His physical features transformed. His eyes seemed to bulge. His whole demeanor changed; he appeared to have enormous energy. His body seemed to grow before my eyes, becoming sturdier. His features changed remarkably: wider cheek bones, burlier, his expression solemn and serious. I could only believe it was John the Baptist. In Entity, Medium João dove into the water and swam, staying under for perhaps two minutes. Medium João himself cannot swim. When he surfaced, his hand was clenched around a large fish. The Entity dove back into the water and came up a few minutes later, just as João unincorporated. His features returned to those of Medium João. He still clutched the sizeable fish, which was now mangled from the pressure of his hand. He told me that at other times, when this particular Entity had incorporated in a river, many fish had died due to the enormous power of the energy.

A group of women washing clothes downriver that day saw many dead fish floating by. Medium João told me he was not permitted to divulge the identity of the Entity. I admit this phenomenon befuddles me; I don't understand it. Others may think I am fabricating the story, but as Medium João says, "It is all true." I like to believe that those fish were liberated into a higher rebirth.

I came as a skeptic and left a believer. You can talk to my wife; she will confirm all of this and tell you how I have changed. We have witnessed so many healings, and she has a much better memory for detail. Every six to eight weeks, I travel to the Casa to serve in the current room as a Casa medium, consult with the Entities, and visit my friend.

▲

PARALYZED FROM THE WAIST DOWN
José Ribeiro

José is a medium in the surgery current room. His beautiful melodious voice can be heard as he prays and leads the current. He owns a general store near the Casa.

José was living in the State of Para when he joined the Brazilian Navy in the early 1980s. On November 19, 1992, while stationed in Rio de Janeiro, he and a colleague were moving equipment when José felt his legs go numb. He also felt a great pain down his left side. José collapsed and was rushed to the hospital. Tests showed a herniated disk at T8 and T9. He was flown to the Naval Hospital in Belem and then to the Naval Hospital of Brasília. The specialists concluded that his case was inoperable. After three months of rehabilitation at the Sara Kubitchek Hospital, he returned home to his wife and daughter. He was paralyzed from the waist down.

José Ribeiro relates:

I had a dream that I arrived at a healing sanctuary and was told to bypass the line and go straight into a certain room. It was vivid and stuck in my memory. I had heard about the Casa. My brother, who lives in Brasília, believed only science could cure me, but he reluctantly took my photo before the Entity. He was told to give me three bottles of blessed water and bring me to the Casa. I began passing clots of blood in my urine within an hour of taking the water.

Against my family's wishes, I convinced my brother to bring me to the Casa in December 1994. It was pouring rain, and we just managed to fit in at the very edge of the main hall. The Entity came down from the dais where he was operating, parted the crowd, and came up directly to me. He took my hand in his and said, "It took you a long time, but you are finally here, filho. Can you stay for three days? I will begin your work."

The Entity sent me straight to the surgery room, bypassing the other current rooms, as in my dream. So my healing began: two years of lying on the maca bed and receiving energy. "Filho, you will go through much more pain, but you will get better," said the Entity (St. Ignatius) before performing an invisible operation on me. I was very ill that weekend and all of the following week. My sister was very concerned. I could not keep food down and could only take coconut water and fluids. On Wednesday, she asked if I should be hospitalized. The Entity told her to have patience and that by the end of the week I would be better. I was better and all our doubts were eventually assuaged.

I wanted to buy a plot of land to build a house. That night I had another powerful dream: There was a huge pile of rubble, and I was lying in a hammock at the side of it. The following day, as I went to the Casa in my wheelchair, I noticed to my right a pile of rubble and a "For Sale" sign. You know, I bought the plot very easily and built my bedroom exactly as in the dream. My wife had left me soon after my accident, but I managed to get custody of my daughter. She is here with me. I have expanded my store, providing work for my family and my parents who have also moved here. Through visions and dreams, I have come to understand my karma. I lead a happy and tranquil life, shared with a wonderful companion. I know I am being healed on many levels. I am not walking yet but am very optimistic. I will walk again one day, but if I do not, I will continue to be a happy man.

▲

A DEVOUT SPIRITIST
Euler Nunes de Oliveira

Euler worked in banking until his retirement in 1999. He speaks several languages and has been a devout and practicing Spiritist for forty years. He is a Casa medium and Spiritist teacher. Euler answers all the letters that come to the Casa with a kind word and a few lines of text from the Gospels. Euler has copies of the Gospels in many languages, so he is able to answer the letters with a message in the language of the writer.

Euler tells his story:

I was somewhat skeptical the first time I came to the Casa. I stayed at the back of the room, standing by the line and watching carefully. I asked in my mind whether there actually was an Entity incorporating in John of God. I asked the Entity to please identify himself to me so I would have no doubt of his authenticity. The

Entity incorporated in Medium João's body and announced himself as Dr. Oswaldo Cruz. Then he performed several surgeries.

When the surgeries were completed, the Entity turned his back and began to leave the hall to go into the current room. As he approached the doorway into the current room, he paused, turned around, and came up to where I was standing. The Entity fixed me with his gaze and asked for a pen and paper. He signed the paper and said, "I am Dr. Oswaldo Cruz. You can verify my signature from my days in public office." Smiling broadly, he turned and left to resume his healing work. In this way, the question I held in my mind was answered. So began my work at the Casa.

Here is the piece of paper with his signature. I have never told this story to anyone before. You may borrow the paper and have it scanned for your book. It is the truth. (This signature has been compared to official documents signed by Dr. Cruz in his lifetime and has been verified.)

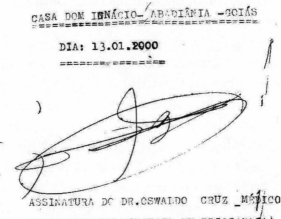

CASA DOM IGNÁCIO_ ABADIÂNIA _GOIÁS

DIA: 13.01.2000

ASSINATURA DC DR.OSWALDO CRUZ _MÉDICO
E PREFEITO DE SOROCABA_SP,PSICOGRAFA-
DA PELO MEDIUM:JOÃO TEXEIRA FARIA EM
ABADIÂNIA-GO-QUINTA FEIRA_13.01.2000.
PEDIU QUE FÔSSE CONFIRMADA A ASSINA-
TURA DC PREFEITO À ÉPOCA.

Signature of Dr. Oswaldo Cruz

▲

A SOUL'S PURPOSE
Heather Cumming

I was born in Brazil, where my Scottish parents managed a cattle ranch in the interior of the country. A trip to the next farm or village was at least a two-hour ride away, yet these great distances fostered a deep sense of kinship among families, a sense of community that deeply resonated with me. Riding the range with the wranglers who worked the land and tended the livestock taught me the importance of living in harmony with nature; the local shamans educated me in native healing traditions. Traditional schooling began at home by my mother, and I attended boarding school in São Paulo and high school in Scotland. However, boarding schools felt alien, and I was uncomfortable in an environment that was cold and devoid of love. Homesick for Brazil, I returned to my beloved home at sixteen; at thirty I married and moved to the States. Still longing for a more spiritual life, I studied shamanism and eventually established a healing practice.

In the summer of 2000, my son and I visited family in the interior of Brazil. Part of my shamanic healing practice involved leading tours to the Amazon to visit Brazilian tribal shamans. While preparing for one of these expeditions, I heard about John of God and instantly felt drawn to visit there. I had never before heard of John of God, but I experienced a "body knowing" as I read a book about him. Shortly afterwards, I was asked to take a small group of people to the Casa for healing. My son and I boarded a bus, traveled throughout the night, and went before the Entity Dr. Augusto the following morning. I had a profound recognition that all of the paths in my life had led me to this expansive moment. After years of yearning, I had found my spiritual home in Abadiânia. I knew I'd found my true calling in this lifetime.

Standing before the Entity known as Dr. Augusto, I wept uncontrollably as memories flooded my being. I thought, *What is unconditional love?* The answer had eluded me all of my life.

"Why are you crying, filha?" the Entity asked.

"I have never experienced such love Father," I said, sobbing.

He reached behind me, took my son Ben's hand in his, and wrote a prescription. Then we both sat in current.

A surge of energy washed over me as I felt a hand inside my body, squeezing and lifting my lung. The pain was similar to having a tooth extracted—a familiar feeling of "pulls and tugs" after receiving anesthesia. I smelled ether and vividly re-experienced a childhood memory of having my tonsils removed.

The next day, at the Entity's request, Sebastian took me on stage to watch a surgery. Mesmerized, I observed Dr. Augusto use a paring knife to perform an abdominal hernia and eye surgery on a man. After the surgery was completed, he instructed me to have five crystal bed sessions and then visit the sacred waterfall. I asked if I could bring small groups to the Casa so they, too, could experience his healing power.

"Bring groups as large as you wish," Dr. Augusto replied.

I felt unsteady as another surge of energy ran through my body, and I reached to Sebastian for support. But it was too late; I immediately collapsed, surrendering to the healing power of Dr. Augusto's blessing. Later, I awoke in the infirmary, where volunteer nurses offered me Casa holy water. In the bed opposite my own was the man who had received surgery, eating Casa soup. He said his hernia no longer hurt and his vision was now perfect. Twenty minutes later, feeling totally energized, I was taken by one of the mediums to the sacred waterfall. I entered the water in silence, with deep gratitude for the healing and blessings I had received.

I have been given countless transformative gifts in my life since my first visit to the Casa. I would like to share a powerful story that demonstrates how all aspects of our lives are taken care of by the Entities.

Two days before I was to meet with my group in Abadiânia, I received word that my daughter was very ill. I was torn between wanting to rush to her side and fulfilling my responsibilities as a group leader. I will never forget my daughter's categorical command when I phoned home: "You must stay at the Casa; you have a group arriving. You can do more for me there than coming home. If you leave now I will refuse to see you. Take care of your group."

On that first Casa day, Sebastian asked me to assist with opening prayers. Sensing my distress, he took my hand and led me to the current room, saying, "Something is deeply troubling you; sit here." A few minutes later, he brought me a glass of passion fruit juice. I sat and wept quietly, focusing on my daughter. Suddenly a hand drew me to my feet, and I found myself looking into the eyes of the Entity, who said, "I don't want to see you like this! You do not need to tell me why you are crying. I know. Before you ask for help for your daughter, I am here to tell you that we are taking care of her. You must not worry. She will be very well. You know that all aspects of the lives of the children of this Casa are taken care of. Where is your faith?" He was kind but somewhat gruff.

Astounded and comforted, I was secure in the knowledge that Sasha and our children, all of us, are protected and cared for in every sense. The Entities love us equally and unconditionally. I have been blessed with an exquisite life. It is a privilege to walk these intimate journeys with fellow seekers—witnessing and bonding as we grow, change, and heal. As the Entity promised, Sasha is indeed doing very well. She graduated from college and is enjoying a rich and full life. I am deeply proud of her and honor her courage, hard work, and commitment to her path.

I have experienced healing in many ways since my first visit to the Casa, including an ovarian cyst that "disappeared" as promised by the Entity and confirmed by ultrasound examination. Yet my deepest healing comes from fulfilling my role as a daughter of the Casa: a member of the Casa family of mediums, who have devoted their lives to service to the Casa and to John of God's healing mission. For the present, my service is twofold: as an official Casa guide, translating for English- and Spanish-speaking visitors who come to the Casa, and taking groups to the Casa on a regular basis. The other is to assist John of God on his healing mission outside of the Casa, accompanying him on healing trips abroad and translating for him and the Entities.

It is with immense appreciation and gratitude that I offer my life in service to my family, to the Casa, to Medium João, to the Entities, and to God's plan to the best of my abilities, and for the highest good of us all. My intention and prayer is to serve with humility and integrity, and to please be shown how to achieve this.

▲

A PORTRAIT OF HEALING
Karen Leffler

I came from a typical, middle-class American family and enjoyed a comfortable childhood. I was college-bound, intent upon a career as a diplomat, but at seventeen, I suffered a loss so great that my life was completely altered. Motivated by an intense desire to make a difference in the world, I began searching for the true meaning of life and death. I spent many years outwardly searching for spiritual understanding and longed to feel a "pure heart."

In 1972, I spent four months in India studying with the Avatar Satya Sai Baba. I received many profound teachings and blessings during that time. I also received a physical token from this enlightened being: a black moonstone ring, an Ishwara lingam that he materialized especially for me.[1] It was the first time that I had ever experienced unconditional love. On the last day I was at his college in Braindavan, Baba asked me what I wanted, to which I replied, "A pure heart." Once again, he materialized a cube of sweet Indian

---

1. According to Indian myth, the lingam and yoni symbolizes the union of cosmic powers of Lord Shiva and his consort Uma.

sugar, saying, "This will cleanse your heart, but you must work; you must meditate." The wonder and grace of that day was the gift of being witnessed by Baba—of having the opportunity to ask and be heard, and to weep for this profound recognition of Divine Love. After laying my head upon his feet in gratitude (as is the custom in India), I returned home.

Wishing to share this life-changing experience with others, I started a Sai Baba Center and proceeded to "do the work" and share the miracles that I had seen. Yet, as time passed, I found that I could not maintain the constant flow of peace and love I had experienced in his presence. As I look back, I now realize I did not fully understand the profound work needed to cultivate a pure heart.

Married and living in Northern California, in a home my partner and I built, I had suffered from migraines since childhood and physical exhaustion. And while my architectural photography business thrived, I felt an inexplicable longing for something more. A chance meeting with a friend brought me news of a remarkable healer in Brazil. Upon arrival in Abadiânia a few weeks later, I felt I had "come home."

When I came before the Entity, Dr. Augusto, for the first time and looked into his eyes, I felt as if I was looking into the very heart of God. Deeply moved, I stood in line that morning with the same recognition of unconditional love I had experienced in India so many years before. Every denomination, every sect, every color and creed was welcome here. No matter how many people were in line, these extraordinary beings took time to see each of us, prescribing herbs, offering advice, and saying, "I am helping; do not worry; I am helping."

Help came to me as I stood in front of the Entity (Dr. Augusto). My heart pounded as the Casa translator brought me before him. I was told I could ask for anything and everything I wanted. I wanted physical healing yet found myself saying, "I want to know God." The translator asked me if I was truly prepared to receive what I had asked for. Of course I was not. This request completely changed my life. Gradually, I came to understand I had unconsciously been unwilling to do the deep inner work required for such a transformation. I do not remember much of what was said that morning, other than Dr. Augusto's gentle command to "Sit in my current room and go to work." I only remember the deep presence of love and the overwhelming tears of recognition. I was not told how to work; there were no set rules for meditation, contemplation, or prayer. Yet I could feel the Entities working with me, using my inner framework to guide me to those "aha" moments of self-liberation. In current, I began to know aspects of myself long denied. I experienced sorrow, joy, and profound gratitude on my new path of self-discovery. My service had begun.

During my stay, I photographed physical surgeries performed on stage at the Casa. When I looked into the LCD of my digital camera, I noticed light distortions: shafts of light radiating from the crystal on the altar next to Medium João, and other unusual light occurrences. I soon realized the photographs were capturing spirit energy. When I showed them to Sebastian, the secretary of the Casa, he was visibly excited, speaking rapidly in Portuguese. Heather translated for me, explaining that these photographs were a gift from the Entities. Heather told me I had been allowed to capture the essence of the spirits. The Entity asked that the photos be framed and placed in the main hall for all to see. They have become a source of inspiration and tangible proof of the healing energy present at the Casa. Little did I know the immense changes that would occur in my outer life because my inner landscape was changing as a result of sincerely asking the Entities for help. These pictures were the beginning of my healing.

With great happiness for my new life, quite scruffy around the edges birthing into the unknown, I give thanks into the heart of the God. I am deeply grateful for the support the Entities have given me throughout my personal healing journey. After shifting my comfortable life of about fifty years from the West Coast to the East Coast in search of the "Holy Grail," I've met my shadow again and again, and I have learned to love and embrace it. Expanding our consciousness to the subtleties of who we really are is what I wish to give others: to give faith to the doubter, hope to the sick, honor to God and our Higher Self, and to be humbled before the tremendous service of the Entities and this compassionate man, John of God.

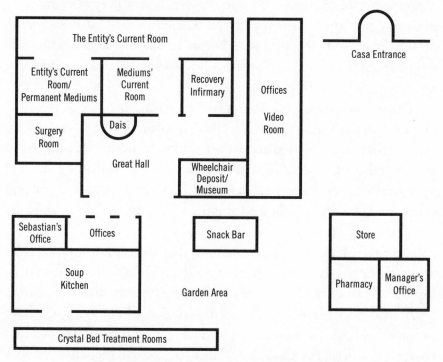

Floor plan of the Casa de Dom Inácio de Loyola

THE CASA DE DOM INÁCIO DE LOYOLA

*Dear João, esteemed friend, Abadiânia is the blessed site
of your illuminated mission and of your peace.*

—Dr. Bezerra de Menezes, channeled by Chico Xavier

After many years in the federal capital of Brasília under the protection of the military, Medium João began to travel from town to town healing the sick. The establishment once again felt threatened. Medium João longed for a sanctuary where people could come to him for treatment.

In 1978, the Entities sent a life-changing message to Medium João through his revered friend and mentor Francisco "Chico" Cândido Xavier. Chico was perhaps the world's most prolific writer on psychic subjects. Virtually unknown in Europe and America, he was cherished by Brazilians and deeply loved by Medium João. Chico devoted his life to helping the poor. He wrote over four hundred spiritual bestsellers, donating all of the proceeds to charity.

Chico received the message *psychographed* (channeled through the written word) by the spirit of Bezerra de Menezes, who directed Medium João to establish a center to practice his charitable works.

Bezerra de Menezes's message designated the minuscule township of Abadiânia as the appropriate location for the sanctuary. It was imperative that there be access to a waterfall nearby. Following these instructions meticulously, Medium João began searching for land.

Medium João has never contemplated leaving Abadiânia, but in 1993 another communication came through Chico Xavier, again incorporating the spirit of Bezerra de Menezes, confirming Abadiânia as the site for Medium João's healing center. The message read, "Prezado João, caro amigo, Abadiânia é o abençoado recinto da sua iluminada missão e de sua paz" (Dear João, esteemed friend, Abadiânia is the blessed site of your illuminated mission and of your peace)—Chico Xavier, Uberaba, September 18, 1993.

Medium João rented a small, one-room, primitive hut near the police station in Abadiânia. Sr. Hamilton Pereira, the mayor of Abadiânia, became friends with João and decided to secure a safe haven for the healer. He went directly to the president of the Medical Association of Goiás, who owned a cattle ranch in the municipality. Sr. Hamilton asked for a guarantee that the Medical Association would allow Medium João to practice his spiritual work, with the stipulation that he build a permanent center in Abadiânia. An accord was reached and his safety assured.

Later that year, Sr. Hamilton's family donated the land where the Casa now stands. The site was in a pasture far from the center of town. A small, humble structure was built, and Medium João was finally allowed to work without interference. There was no electricity in the vicinity at that time. The Casa is located in a beautiful setting overlooking the nearby expanse of hills and valleys, and it is centered over a natural energy vortex formed by quartz crystal bedrock beneath the surface.

The Casa was officially named *Case de Dom Inácio de Loyola* (The House of St. Ignatius of Loyola) in honor of one of the principal Entities who guides Medium João, Dom Inácio de Loyola, or *Dom Inácio*. The colors of the Casa are sky blue and white, following the explicit request of Dom Inácio in a vision to Medium João. Dom Inácio de Loyola was the founder of the Jesuit Order. (The title *Dom* carries more respect than *Mr.* and is similar to *Sir.*)

Sr. Hamilton's mother, Dona Rosinha, built the first pousada for visitors next to the front gates of the Casa. It was named after her and is now known as the *Pousada Santa Rita*.

Medium João lives in Anápolis, thirty-five kilometers (21 miles) from the Casa. He owns two cattle ranches and a partnership in a gold mine and an emerald mine. His impoverished childhood and hard physical labor helped him to mature into a successful business entrepreneur and rancher. He is acutely aware that his spiritual work needs to be supported financially by his business projects. He rarely takes a vacation, because he is on a continuous cycle of work to support his mission. Medium João works at the Casa every Wednesday, Thursday, and Friday. Several times a year, he travels to the affiliate Casa in the south of Brazil and to other states. He departs for these sessions by plane on Friday night and treats the masses on Saturday, Sunday, and Monday, traveling home to resume his duties in Abadiânia on Wednesday. He has also traveled outside of Brazil to many countries, including Peru, Portugal, Germany, America, Greece, and New Zealand, always returning to Abadiânia for the regular Casa sessions.

Medium João possesses a commanding stature. He is six feet tall, with a gentle dignity and sensitivity born out of humility. His clear, blue eyes flash joyously with his work, but they can change color with his incorporation. His physical features also change. For instance, when Dom Inácio incorporates, Medium João limps and reaches for a hand to steady him while he walks. This is because Dom Inácio was wounded by a cannon shot to his leg in the sixteenth century. Dom Inácios's eyes appear much bigger and deeper blue than Medium João's, and there is such a powerful transmission of love that emanates from this Entity that there is rarely a dry eye to be seen when he incorporates. Sometimes, Medium João's hair seems to be thicker or sparser, depending on the spirit who is incorporated. Occasionally, an Entity makes their identity known. More often, they can be identified by their distinct attributes, manner, and speaking styles.

The Entities have their own unique personalities. The more frequently incorporated Entities can be recognized and often identify themselves. Dr. Augusto, for example, announces himself with authority: "I am Dr. Augusto de Almeida!" Other Entities from Dr. Augusto's phalange will often honor him as they incorporate by announcing in old-fashioned language: "Hail to Dr. Augusto!" Dr. Augusto seems to be highly evolved and much honored and respected by members of his group. One Entity asked Karen to take his picture, and when Heather asked, "What is your name, Father?" his answer was, "Love!"

Another time, someone wanted to know the Entity's name. When asked, he answered, "It doesn't matter what my name is. I am of Dom Inácio's phalange. All the filhos of the Casa have the honor of seeing Dom Inácio. I am not worthy to kneel at his feet." This was surely a highly evolved soul who cared not for recognition. We are not sure exactly who all of the thirty-five or more Entities are, but Chapter 9 offers what little is known about the Entities who incorporate most frequently. Female Entities also incorporate into Medium João's body, but in this case, the tone of voice does not change. At various times, the Entities interchange, entering and leaving Medium João's body several times during a single session. After the initial jolt of the incorporation, the transitions are seamless and simultaneous, and observers are usually not aware when they occur.

Heather speaks about a specific interaction with the Entities:
Once I was discussing Lyme's disease in America with the incorporated Entity. I said this illness is carried by a small tick and was becoming epidemic. Adding that I knew many people suffering

from this disease, including children, I asked for help. The Entity said he would have a special lotion prepared and show me how to apply it. He asked me to come back the following week.

When I went before the Entity a week later and asked him about the special lotion, he merely told me to sit in current. Then I realized that this particular Entity was not familiar with my request. It must have been Dr. Oswaldo Cruz who had spoken to me previously, and today's incorporation was a different Entity.

On my next trip to the Casa, I brought a photograph of a person afflicted with Lyme's disease before the Entity. As I approached, I thought to myself, *Dr. Augusto is the one incorporated, but it is Dr. Cruz who helps me with this issue.* I showed the photo to the Entity and explained my concerns about Lyme's disease. The Entity gave me a prescription and waved me on.

I was no more than three steps away when he called me back. The Entities had switched, and Dr. Oswaldo Cruz was now incorporated. "You are right, filha. It is me, not Dr. Augusto, who is helping you with this. I am going to give you a recipe. Rub it on the skin like this (he showed me how to do it) and tell no one of the ingredients." He had me wait while he sent for Antão. Then he gave Antão a list of herbs to be found in the fields and gave careful directions as to how to make up a liter of the preparation. I cannot give the specific recipe because certain phrases, prescriptions, and mantras must be kept confidential so as not to dissipate the power and sanctity of the information.

• • •

Medium João suffered a stroke in 1987. This left him partially paralyzed down one side. His eyes and hands appeared atrophied, hardened, and somewhat deformed. However, during incorporation, his body would appear as healthy as it did prior to the stroke. One day, the Entity incorporated and performed surgery on Medium João's body, cutting him on the left side below the breast bone. Afterward, Medium João's body reverted back to a normal state of health and he remains the same today. Medium João is sickened and becomes faint at the sight of blood, which is surely confirmation that he is not present during incorporation—not even on this occasion when "he" operated on himself while in-entity.

In July 2004, Medium João asked his trusted friend Hamilton to take over the position of Casa manager. The Casa is extremely fortunate to have Sr. Hamilton in this capacity. He had previously pursued a long and successful political career, and he was well employed and living in the city of Goiânia when he answered his friend's call for help and moved back to Abadiânia.

Sr. Hamilton speaks about Medium João:

Abadiânia owes its development and prosperity to this extraordinary man. The much-needed progress and growth of the town is due solely to the presence of Medium João. There has been an influx of new residents, who have built homes and started new businesses. Medium João supports many projects in this town, especially the police force and security. In the past two years alone, he has donated four motorbikes to the civil police. He generously donates to the needy, offering care packages throughout the region and funds for education and building projects. He also provides secure employment at the Casa, the soup kitchens, and on his farms. This year, he opened yet another soup kitchen located near the town hall. I understand this kind, generous, and complex man, and I think it is important for me to stay by his side. I accepted this position because I honor and love my friend. We have known each other for over thirty years. His mission is not an easy one, and I hope to alleviate some of the burden.

Spiritual Soup

Aparecida Rosa Reis and her husband, Mario, arrived at the Casa for treatment in 1978. Aparecida was gravely ill and emaciated. She had been diagnosed with cancer of the ovaries and uterus, and she was constantly hemorrhaging. She faced a dismal future. The Entities asked her to remain for an undetermined period of time to be cured. She rented a small room near the Casa and cooked meals for herself and her husband.

In time, she began sending meals to Medium João, who enjoyed the food and asked to meet her. (The Entity was treating her, not Medium João, who had no personal memory of her healing sessions.) João insisted that he would supply the ingredients for her meals. As Aparecida healed and got stronger, João gave her bigger pans, larger food supplies, and invited her to cook for the members of the current. Her food was quite good, and she combined a healthy variety of meat, chicken, rice, beans, and vegetables. Her cooking was so delicious, in fact, that one day the current members overate and were sluggish and sleepy for the afternoon session. The Entity decreed the midday meal was to be substituted for a substantial soup that would be more digestible. Since then, soup has been served after the morning sessions.

The Entities' parting words before they leave Medium João's body are always an invitation to make sure everyone has soup and blessed water. However, the soup is not limited to those attending the Casa. It is available for anyone who is hungry and wants to eat. A full lunch is offered to all of the Casa staff, and extra is always made for volunteers and Medium João's guests. He cannot bear the thought of anyone going hungry, so plenty of food is always available. There is a cook whose sole job is to make the soup. The vegetables are peeled on Tuesday mornings, and volunteers are always welcome to help. Each morning, the cook checks the lines in the great hall and the current rooms for an approximate number. On St. Ignatius's anniversary, for example, she will double or triple the amount. The soup cook finds it remarkable that when she makes the soup with the exact same ingredients at home it does not taste the same. The soup is specially imbued with energy by the Entities, and this is another aspect of the healing process. The Entities ask all guests to rest quietly in their rooms and not leave the hotels for twenty-four hours after receiving spiritual surgery. When planning a trip to the Casa, be sure to let your pousada or hotel know when you are resting after surgery. Soup will be brought to your room so you will not miss a day.

Aside from the soup offered at the Casa, Medium João distributes over 80,000 bowls of soup to the poor every year from his soup kitchens in other locations in Brazil.

Medium João Teixeira de Faria concludes:
Over twenty-eight years ago, I established the House of Dom Inácio on the soil of Abadiânia—this blessed Earth where God placed me to accomplish my mission. I do not cure anybody. The one who cures is God. I am merely an instrument in his Divine hands. God, in his infinite kindness and compassion, permits the Entities of Light to provide you, my brothers and sisters, with healing and comfort.

I have been a gem prospector, and I know that the precious stone needs to suffer the process of cutting and polishing in order to reveal its beauty. Seeing a gem in its raw state, one would not give it any value, but once polished, its magnificence is revealed. Every son and daughter is a rare diamond of creation, but they must be polished, implying pain and suffering, in order to realize their higher mission and consciousness.

The world passes through great transformations, consequently generating great suffering, so we must put our faith and trust in the One Supreme Being who is our God.

In conclusion, I give to you as a message the words of Christ from the Gospel of John (chapter 15, verse 12): "This is my commandment, that you love one another as I have loved you."

João de Deus was born João Teixeira de Faria in Cachoeira da Fumaça, Goiás (now Cachoeira de Goiás), Brazil. Here is an early photograph of Medium João at about 17 years of age in the early days of his healing mission.

Medium João in his mid-thirties escorting his mother, Dona Iuca, to church. He was especially devoted to his mother.

Ana Keyla Teixeira Lorenço, Medium João's wife, has dedicated her life to supporting Medium João, his mission, and the Casa.

Medium João eats watermelon and drinks coconut water at a roadside vendor in his hometown of Itapaçi, a four hour journey from Abadiânia.

Medium João's childhood home

Medium João sewing and ironing his clothes at his home in Anápolis

Medium João mending and sewing Ana's clothes on a sewing machine that he had bought back after selling it thirty-five years ago

The lush tropical gardens at the Casa where visitors meditate in tranquil surroundings

View from the Casa overlook where visitors enjoy sunsets and listen to the call of Brazilian birds

At the request of Dr. Augusto de Almeida, the sacred waterfall, Cachoeira de Lázaros, near the Casa grounds was photographed despite its "no photographs" protocol so that everyone could see its radiating energy.

The Entity's chair where Medium João sits as
millions file past him for healing

Medium João holds Martin's hand as he incorporates the being that will use his body for healing.

During the incorporation of an Entity, Medium João's body begins to shudder as consciousness leaves his body and the Entity enters, ready to perform healings for the day's session.

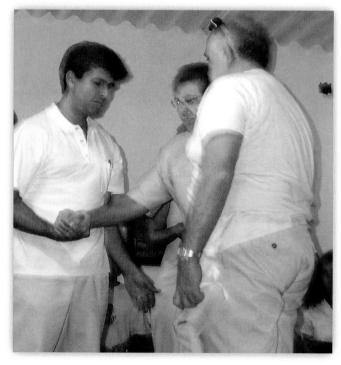

Dr. Augusto noted that this spirit photo "shows the power of this crystal, which was mined twelve meters underground."

Heather Cumming translates for Medium João and a Casa visitor holding his baby. This photograph is not out of focus but captures the swirls of energy used for healing.

The triangle in the Great Hall where people lay their heads, pray, and place messages and pictures. As visitors rest their heads on the triangle, they can feel heaven touching earth as a portal opens and light pours down.

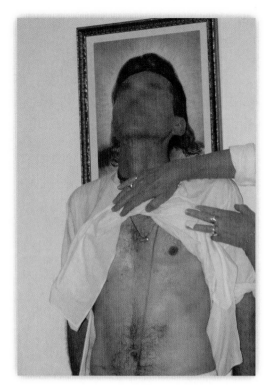

This is the first in a series of three photographs that trace energy coming through during surgery. In this photo, the man's head covers the face of Jesus as Heather lifts his shirt in preparation for surgery.

As the Entity begins the surgical procedure, a yellow light radiates from the painting of Jesus behind the patient.

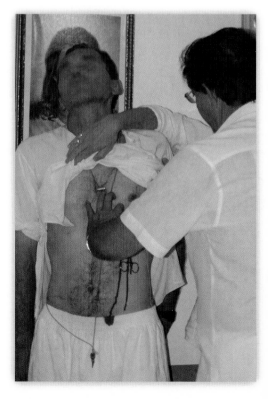

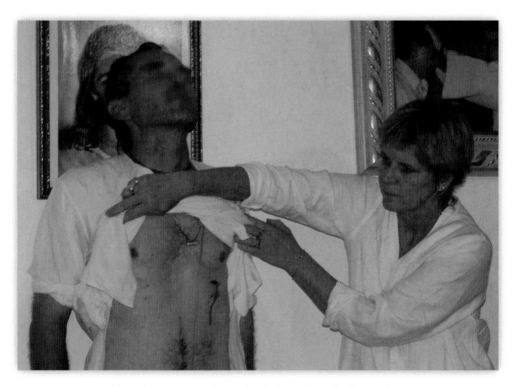

Note the color over the patient's head that slowly recedes
as the surgery is completed.

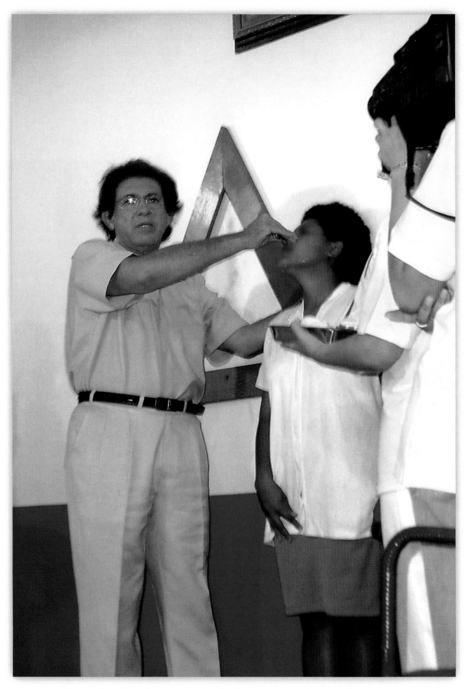

The patient's calm expression indicates she is in no pain, despite the Entity having just inserted and twisted a 6-inch surgical Kelly clamp into her nose. The clamp had beforehand been wrapped in cotton and dipped in holy water.

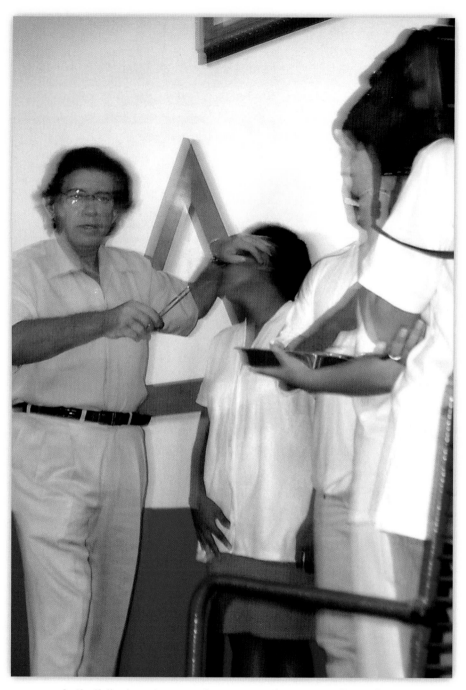

As the Kelly clamp is removed one can see the energy radiating from the Entity's head and hands. The Entities confirmed that up to nine different ailments can be addressed in this type of procedure.

Francis Xavier washing his hands after surgery. Oftentimes the blood disappears before he has time to wash his hands.

The Entity Dr. Augusto
intent on his work

Sirlei Lerner's altar painting of Dom Inácio hangs above the Entity's chair. See Sirlei's story in chapter 10.

This painting is a likeness of Dr. Augusto de Almeida in his past life. He transitioned into the spiritual world in 1908. See chapter 9, on "Spiritism and the Entities."

Approximately 2,500 people waiting to be seen by the Entity in Atlanta, Georgia, in April 2006.

The Entity's current room in Atlanta, Georgia, where people sat to receive and give energy for healing.

THE GREAT HALL AND THE CURRENT ROOMS

Selfishness causes us to see competitors in everyone.
Fraternity finds brothers and sisters in all.

—Chico Xavier

The extraordinary abilities and dedication of Medium João and the phalange of compassionate spirits he incorporates have been scientifically tested and studied.[1] Television documentaries, media presentations, and books have brought awareness of this miraculous phenomenon to millions, who might otherwise never have heard of him. Thousands of people travel from all over the world to seek his help and comfort. They come from all walks of life and have all kinds of ailments, and many have been declared terminal or incurable. Many people seeking spiritual growth and transformation also come. A steady stream of doctors, scientists, quantum physicists, politicians, professors, actors, and filmmakers from all over the world have been treated by the Entities. The

---

1. Dr. Alfredina Arlete Savaris, post-graduate thesis, "*Curas Paranormais Realizadas por João Teixeira de Faria*"; Robert Pellegrino-Estrich, *The Miracle Man*, chapter 11, "Scientific Observations."

famous and the ordinary, people of all colors, creeds, and religions are seen without favoritism.

THE GREAT HALL

The central building of the Casa is a large meeting hall. On Wednesdays, Thursdays, and Fridays, everyone gathers in this "Great Hall" at 8:00 A.M. and 2:00 P.M. wearing white clothing, because white enhances the visibility of the auric field. Black or other dark colors make it more difficult for the Entities to view our bodies and perform their healing work.

Sebastian begins by leading a recitation of the Lord's Prayer. This universal prayer serves as a tool for centering and focus. The group prayer creates a current that expands and nourishes everyone present. Each person is a filament of this creative life force, referred to as *Light, Prana, Chi,* or *Ki.* Each person is like a single thread of light. A hundred threads become a strong chain or *current of light.* The word *corrente* in Portuguese means "chain," or "current," as in electricity. All of those praying and meditating together are links in this great chain. At the Casa, this is called *holding current.* When everyone is focused in their prayers and meditations, the Entities easily draw upon this energy for healing.

Hold the intention of love and the highest good for all when you sit in the current room. If you feel your mind drifting, simply repeat this intention. Do not open your eyes or cross your arms and legs. The Entities feel the drop in energy when you do this, and it breaks the chain of consciousness, making it more difficult for the Entities to do their work. When the current becomes unfocused or weak, it can cause pain to those undergoing treatment. It also causes physical pain in the body of Medium João and the Casa mediums. A strong, focused current carries each of us into a state of higher consciousness. All of our individual differences are transcended as we come together in a state of Oneness. In this way, we all partici-pate in co-creation: an open, ongoing collaboration with the Entities wherein our focus is on the single intention of service for the highest good of all.

Soon Sebastian calls for those who were previously told they would undergo spiritual surgery to form a line. He escorts them into the surgery room adjacent to the Great Hall, where they sit on long benches or rest on stretchers with their eyes closed. Following the guidance of the Casa mediums, they prepare themselves for invisible or physical surgery.

While reciting the Prayer of Caritas, Medium João incorporates an Entity—usually in his current room and sometimes in the Great Hall. Entering into a full trance, his ordinary consciousness is suspended and his body becomes a vessel for the Entities. When he is "in-entity," his stature, gaze, and speech are markedly different from the man, João. Everyone who is present feels the love and power flowing through him, affirming his benign possession by the spirit Entity. As John of God constantly reminds us, "I do not cure anybody; God heals. I am merely the vessel." After a period of about ten minutes, the Entity recites a prayer in Portuguese, enters the surgery room, and declares, "In the name of God the surgery is complete."

The Entity then returns to the second current room and takes his seat on a wooden rocking chair. Next to him is a large crystal sitting on a simple table that serves as an altar. The table also has a drawer that holds the instrument trays for the physical surgeries. The Entity picks up his pen and begins the day with the request, "Bring in the filhos of the second line." The line is quickly gathered and counted, and people proceed to the first current room.

FIRST CURRENT ROOM: The Medium School

The first current room is often referred to as *medium school*, where participants learn to enhance their ability to channel the light and hold the space for themselves and others as they receive and give energy. The Casa mediums use imagery and prayer to assist visitors in focusing their intention and deepening the spiritual understanding involved in this work. There are always two permanent mediums in this room. They live in the surrounding area, and having been healed, they return to do service. There are approximately sixty permanent mediums at the Casa at any one time giving service by holding the current.

Walking through the first current room is like going into a spiritual washing machine; everyone is bathed in spiritual light as they walk through. Each person's energetic field is cleansed on all levels as they begin to attune to the high frequency of the current. This is the time for each person to look into their heart and state their intention for healing. It is the time to ask the Entities to go to the root cause of whatever is blocking ultimate health and vitality. With this simple request for assistance, the Entities are given permission to begin their spiritual work in collaboration with each person's desire for wholeness. Healing does not take place while standing in line or standing before the Entity: It takes place while sitting in current with the eyes closed and the mind and soul focused on connecting with Source. Each of us is empowered through direct revelation by the Entities as we sit in current. This is the opportunity offered to us by the Entities so we can develop individual discernment through prayer and meditation: being still and connecting to our inner wisdom. The information needed for our healing comes in various forms: visions (clairvoyance), sound (clairaudience), colors, fragrances, vibrations, and even memories. As we learn to listen and trust this communication, the Entities' guidance is established within us as we reconnect to our own Divinity. This expanded consciousness is the foundation for healing, and many people return from the Casa with an inner peace that was not known before. Each person has learned, through direct experience, how to unburden themselves of their ailments, both physical and emotional.

SECOND CURRENT ROOM: The Entity's Current Room

One by one, each person passes before the Entity and is scanned by the spirits who will perform healing. For some, the effect is immediate—for others, healing unfolds over time. Additional visits are required for most people. Each person is viewed as a hologram when standing before the Entity, who sees him as energy. This gives the Entity instant access to every aspect of the person's physical, emotional, and spiritual history, because illness is first a "dis-ease" of the spirit. With permission, and only for the highest good, the Entities begin the healing process on all levels. We must take responsibility for our actions. It is through our willingness to trust and surrender that we heal. As Medium João says, "There is no magic here. Here we practice the Love of God."

The Entity may prescribe herbs, invite you to stay in his current room, send you to the first current room, or prepare you for surgery. This preparation may include meditating in the current rooms, crystal bed therapy, or going to the waterfall (see chapter 7). A person's continued presence in the Entity's current room is only by the request of the Entity. Usually the invitation is effective for a twenty-four-hour period. Visitors then return to the second-time line to seek further instructions. Casa mediums are often told to sit in his current for extended periods of time. Sometimes, the Entity may ask you to sit in the surgery current or the first current room. Each of these rooms is equally important and vital in maintaining the balance, harmony, and high frequency of energy needed for healing. To honor the Entity and ensure highest healing, it is important to follow the protocols by going into whichever current room he indicates.

The current room is a spiritual banquet that should be respected by diligent adherence to the standards set by the Entities. Concentration in the rooms must be kept stable, and all visitors are asked to follow the various protocols. On one occasion, the Entity stood up, moved into the small surgery room, sat on a hard bench, and resumed attending to the line and writing prescriptions. When asked if there was a problem in his room, he replied, "No one is concentrating in that other room. Eyes are open and there is no focus, so I will work from here. The energy is stronger."

Once you have met the Entities, they will fine-tune you wherever you might be, regardless of which current room you sit in. The work continues when you are in your hotel room and after you return home. You can always resume your connection with the Entities through meditation and prayer. You are never alone, because the spiritual family of the Casa lovingly holds you anywhere in the world.

CONNECTING TO THE CURRENT

A high frequency of positive energy is transmitted when people gather together in the current rooms. The positive thoughts and prayers of the mediums mutually support the group, as everyone comes into resonance and coherence with divine consciousness. Rather than focusing on illness or pain, focus on an image of wellness. Visualize yourself whole and complete—dancing, playing, singing, or running along the beach—all the things you would like to be doing. Use all of your senses to create a mental image, a vision of your desires already made manifest. Energize your mental image and balance any disharmony by focusing on something that brings you joy. You will begin to smile and feel an inner exhilaration. It is this inner elation that raises consciousness and frequency into divine resonance. Once you are in vibrational harmony with the Divine, focus on receiving and giving divine energy. Declare that your healing is already happening. Positive thoughts and images greatly enhance the current and help the Entities, who draw on this positive, high-frequency energy for their work.

The current is like an orchestra playing an exquisite symphony. The Entity is the conductor, leading us as we play together in perfect attunement. But when someone crosses their arms or legs, or opens their eyes, the harmony is disrupted. The tempo is lost. If you become uncomfortable, hold yourself with love and compassion, quietly leave and go out to the garden, and sit on a bench or under a tree. Mindful of the fresh air, the fragrances of the land, and the singing birds, reconnect with the current through nature. Close your eyes and visualize yourself being refreshed under a cool waterfall of light that flows through all of your cells, linking you to the current. In this way, the next time you sit in the current rooms you will once more be a finely tuned instrument. Keep in mind that any discomfort you experience may have been activated by the Entities in order to help you get in touch with your emotional pain and release it.[2]

SURGERY ROOM

When you are invited to have surgery, it is usually performed in the surgery room. There are two types of spiritual surgery: invisible and physical. A body is not physically touched during invisible surgery, and most people elect this option. The Entities follow certain criteria for physical surgery. It is offered to people under fifty-three and over eighteen years of age. Those who suffer from epilepsy, heart conditions, or diabetes, or anyone undergoing chemotherapy and radiation treatments, are not eligible. There is no difference between physical and invisible surgery at the Casa. Those who volunteer for physical surgery often state they need tangible proof of the healing process. Up to nine different surgeries can be performed simultaneously by the Entitites. Physical surgeries at the Casa may include entering the nasal cavity with a hemostat that is clamped to a cotton wad and dipped in blessed water. Alternatively, the eye may be scraped with a knife. This type of surgery is not only for treating an eye ailment, because the eye is representative of the entire body system. Thus, scraping the eye can heal other parts of the body. The Entities also physically remove tumors during surgery. The person receiving these treatments does not feel any pain.

2. For readers who are intending to go to the Casa, please refer to chapter 7, "Tools, Modalities, and Prayers," for more tips on holding current.

FIRST TIME, SECOND TIME, AND REVISION LINES

The *first-time line* is for people who are meeting the Entity for the first time. The *second-time line* is for those who have previously visited the Entity. Always return to the second-time line after your first session with the Entity. If you have not physically been to the Casa before, but someone else has presented your picture to the Entity, then you are considered as "having been seen and attended to." Thus, you should join the second-time line on your first visit to the Casa. The 8:00 A.M. and 2:00 P.M. lines are for those who have already passed before the Entity and were asked to return at that specific time. There are many reasons for this. A different Entity may need to see a particular person, or the Entity may be moving the line along to expedite the work and protect Medium João's body, which may be tiring. Finally, there is the *revision line* for people who have received either physical or spiritual surgery and are returning after eight days for their review before the Entities. This procedure allows the Entities to see how the healing has progressed, remove any sutures, and adjust the treatment. This is similar to postoperative checkups by medical doctors. The entities remind us that they work in conjunction with Western medicine and require that patients follow conventional medical protocol and not stop any treatment prescribed by medical doctors, who are called *earth doctors* by the Entities.

A DAY IN THE CURRENT ROOMS

I am giving health, but only God gives life.

—Dr. Augusto de Almeida

Heather relates personally witnessed healing stories from her diary:
I sat surrogate surgery for a friend this morning. The Entity told me to sit in his current and focus on my friend. I began to pray, asking for purification and cleansing, thanking the Entities, and asking to

be a clear channel of God's healing light. I began to focus on my friend as I held a small, white piece of paper in my hand with her name and address. I offered gratitude for the healing I was certain she was already receiving. Energy began to flood into my hand, and I felt a deep surge of emotion as I continued to focus on her.

At that moment, Dr. Augusto de Almeida incorporated and announced himself. I heard him talking but it seemed very far away. The energy in the room was potent, and surges of energy passed through my body and into my hand. I saw brilliant colors washing through my friend. I became aware of the Entity standing in front of me, just as he announced the surgery session was complete.

Three years ago, Dr. Augusto had marked my friend's photograph with an "X," indicating that she should come to Brazil. The Entity, on seeing her photograph again, twice affirmed that she *must* come to the Casa. I felt it was Dr. Augusto. He remained there for about four minutes, and then he said, "Intention and focus." Again, surges of energy passed through my body and into my hand—brilliant colors washed over me.

"How is she? Would you like to call her now or later? It would be better to do so later. You can continue to send her energy. With Love," he said, his voice emphatic, but with a very loving cadence. "Take her three bottles of water. Her illness has been incubating for ten years, twelve years even. There is no magic practiced here. Her healing will take time. Nourishment is very important. Wash the leaves (vegetables) and fruits well before eating—nobody does this correctly. There exists a hospital above the Casa, and the Entities are helping everyone, not just those marked for surgery. All the filhos and the mediums are receiving energy. I am giving health. But only God gives life. Do you know who I am? I am Dr. Augusto de Almeida. You may call in the children of the second-time line."

As he moved to take his seat, I wept, flooded with love. I trust the Entities can hear the expression of gratitude in our hearts that goes beyond the inadequacy of words.

I stood up to help Tânia, one of the Casa mediums and leader of the current room. Tânia was in a car accident that should have left her paralyzed. She arrived at the Casa suffering excruciating back pain after complex spinal surgery. Now she is in service, while at the same time receiving healing. She *stands* near the Entity and helps with anything he needs. Her mediumship is advanced, and she sees and senses energy astutely. This position carries a lot of responsibility. There are other volunteers, some who live away from Abadiânia, who also have this position. They interchange from time to time. After the current session is over, the leader (in this case Tânia) works in another room, carefully washing the instruments and following the Entity's directives. She takes the basket with the photos and slips of paper that are collected from beneath the triangles, where many people pray, to a special room where they receive further attention from the Entities. Tânia also prepares the room energetically with prayers each day.

The day continues:

It was another long morning for the Entity and Medium João's body. Six buses came from the south, over thirty hours of traveling for the passengers. So many healings took place. The quiet consultations of the Entity were sporadically interrupted by resounding crashes as walking sticks and crutches were removed by the Entity and thrown across the room. Miraculous moments and constant grace flowed in the three and half hours of current. At the time, it was vibrant and unforgettable, but unless recorded soon, it becomes dreamlike and surreal.

At some point, a woman with a large, hard growth on her right wrist approached the Entity. The Entity (Dr. José Valdivino) called for his instruments. Tânia took the instrument tray and handed me the cotton wool container to hold in one hand and the blessed water container in the other. He motioned for us to stand to his left while he gently massaged the area of the growth. He reached for the scalpel and broke it free from the sterile paper. He took it and began cutting into the growth, which had been hard and stone-like earlier. Laying down the scalpel, he squeezed the area and told us to watch as pus poured out and then blood and lumps of tissue. He wiped it clean with the towel and asked for surgical tape. Tânia collected the tape container and began to pull out the tape.

"That tape is no longer sterile," Dr. Valdivino said. "Did you know that only Medium João's hands and body are sterile?"

Tânia offered bandages, but as she removed them from the paper he again declared they were not sterile. "What will you do now?" he asked. We were both mystified because the normal procedure is for Tânia to hand him the tape. There was an awkward silence as he watched us, waiting for an answer.

"May I hold the top of the tape container, hand it to you, and then you draw the tape?" I said.

"Yes, that will work, and now give me some gauze, filha Tânia." He cut some gauze and placed it on the wound, which was now completely flat, the inch-long cut barely visible. He asked me to rub my thumb, index, and second fingers together for a few seconds. He then placed his index finger on the point of my index finger. "There, now your finger is sterilized and you can hold this gauze in place." He cut the tape, and I removed my index finger from the wound as he placed the tape on the gauze. I offered him the bowl of water and towel to wash his hands, noting that the blood that had been on his hand had already disappeared. He smiled and splashed the water as he washed his hands in the bowl.

"Pronto. Acabou. Sentiu dor?" (There. It is finished. Did you feel any pain?) The weeping woman kissed his hands—she had felt absolutely no pain.

Tânia and I assumed the Entity was sending a message to someone, perhaps a doctor who was present in the current room, perhaps a skeptic, informing them that only the Medium's body was sterile. He had made his statements loud and clear for a reason, and certainly to protect Medium João.

During the lunch break, I had the honor of meeting Dona Margarida. She and Sebastian spent an hour telling stories about the "old days."

Dona Margarida shares:

We had to keep moving to flee the authorities when Medium João practiced his work. He spent a lot of time with each person in those days. There were not as many people as there are now. Forty people would take the whole day, with the Entities talking and performing individual surgeries. I miss those days. Today the Entity smiled at me, but it was fleeting. He told me I must never stand in line because I have been with him for so many years. He told Sebastian to bring me up to him at the beginning of the session.

I was the cook in the early days. Sometimes we had only one egg and a little rice for all of us. It was difficult to come up with variety. For a while, we practiced out of a tiny house with a minute kitchen and two rooms in which the Entity worked. Sebastian, do you remember the time the toilets overflowed? There was only one toilet for all those people. Even Medium João carried buckets of the foul-smelling toilet overflow and threw it into the pit. Afterward, he told us to rest while he cooked us the most wonderful lunch. He is a great cook, you know. He can make a meal out of any little scraps, and his rice is the best I have ever eaten.

At night, we would all sleep on the floor on mattresses. "One day," he promised us, "I will find a place on a quiet piece of land where we can work and no one will chase us away." Medium João moved to Abadiânia soon after that. The Casa was in the *mato* (the bush), just like he said. I am so happy to see him now with this big retreat and doing his work in safety and helping so many. His dream has been realized. We never imagined it would turn out like this—no more hiding and poverty. God will continue to help us all. But I do miss the old days and all the fun we had.

Sebastian shares:
I remember when the lines were very long with hundreds of people, many buses, and the attending room was very small. Each surgery was individual, and it took many hours to see everyone. We did not have the infrastructure we have now. The Great Hall was small and there were no seats. It would be filled to capacity, with the lines going all around the gardens. We would start at 8:00 A.M., and at 11:00 A.M. the mediums of the current would change so the first group could eat lunch and rest. The work would continue. Medium João would not stop. Fortunately, his bodily functions are arrested during incorporation, and the Entity feeds his body with sips of coconut water. We would finish very late at night. It's good to have the rest periods we have now. Medium João is older and needs to rest and eat. Still, you see, he gets very little sleep.

Heather shares:
The afternoon session began with opening prayers. Then the Entity took a man who was scheduled for physical surgery by the hand and led him out on the dais. He asked him to lean against the wall in front of the picture of Jesus. I held the man's shirt up. "It's good for you to see this. Watch," the Entity said to me. He drew two fingers down the man's chest and up to his heart in a U-sweep. Instantly the man's chest area broke out in a sweat and his skin tone changed slightly. Next, the Entity took the scalpel from the paper sheath and made a small incision about two inches to the right and below his breast. "Pay attention. Look what I'm doing with the energy." He put two fingers just above the cut and the energy brought down the flow of blood. He took the clamp and clamped the skin. Two swift stitches and the bleeding had stopped. In Karen's series of photos you can see the light changing around the image of Jesus as the surgery proceeds.

The Entity called Martin to use his back as a brace for the next man in line to lean on, while he performed surgery using a scalpel to clear a growth from the man's arm. After he had removed the tumor, he gave the needle and thread to an observer, a dentist, to sew the sutures. The dentist tried and tried to get the needle through the skin. The Entity smiled and said gently, "The energy that creates the anesthesia will begin to wear off. Here I will finish for you." Two swift movements and the sutures were done. The Casa staff, prompt and adept, whisked the man off in a wheelchair to the recovery room. The bleeding had stopped. Blessed water would be applied, and the volunteer nurses would care for him with love and prayers.

Returning to his chair in the current room, the Entity announced, "Bring the children of the second line." And so the afternoon continued: The Entity wrote prescriptions, pausing to give guidance, a smile, a few words of encouragement, and sometimes calling doctors and lawyers to come and witness a healing. Several people who had been cured came up to give thanks. Sebastian brought a stooped, old Japanese-Brazilian woman to the head of the line. She has visited Medium João for many years. He gave her a prescription and announced how long she has been coming to the Casa. The woman was ninety-two years old. She beamed and went to sit quietly in the current.

Toward the end of the session, a woman brought her mother up from the current. She asked the Entity to help her mother because she has so much pain from arthritis that she cannot even cook for herself. The Entity stood up and placed his hands on the mother's shoulders, closed his eyes, and said loudly, "The One who creates the rivers and the trees is healing you now." His body shuddered slightly. He ushered her over to the water jug and told her to pour some water and drink it. "Any pain?" he inquired. She was thrilled to confirm the pain was gone, but she came hurrying back to him. "Now my legs, please," she said. He smiled and placed his hand on her knees. "Now go to work in my current. I am helping you." He resumed his seat and the line continued to pass before him.

Several people handed roses to the Entity, who smiled graciously and gave them to Tânia to distribute to the current members or those coming down the line. Roses that have been held by the Entity seem to last longer, especially if they are put in a vase with blessed water. At the end of the session, the Entity called for the closing prayer and announced he was "going up." He asked God for a good cleansing of all the mediums and the rooms. "Stay in the peace of God," he said quietly. Then Medium João's body shuddered slightly and he walked slowly and stiffly to his room.

▲

HERBS AND PRESCRIPTIONS, A LABOR OF LOVE
Antão

Antão has assisted Medium João for twenty-four years. He is a big man, and he stands watchfully outside the door all day to protect Medium João. He does not leave his post until Medium João has driven off the premises. He creates a tally of how many are in attendance each day and in which line they are standing. He leads each line to the Entity and tells him how many are behind him in the line. These numbers are important to the Entities for reasons we do not understand. Sometimes the Entity will say, "Antão, don't you know how to count? There were many more people in this line than your tally." It's almost impossible to count the number of people in the lines as they come and go, and Antão takes the gentle chiding at the inaccurate numbers in his stride, smiling broadly.

Antão talks about the prescribed herbs after surgery:
The herbal prescriptions used to be a liquid. We would mix the preparation in large vats and bottle it in pint-size glass containers. Production was a continuous labor of love. All the bottles would

be lined up on shelves. The pharmacy mediums are trained by the Entities. When they bring the prescription and the bottle together, the liquids—or the Passiflora herbal capsules we use now—are imbued with energy uniquely for each person. The preparation changes color, consistency, and even fragrance. Having made the preparation ourselves from the same batch of herbs, we would always be astounded that upon opening our personal bottles, each would be unique and different. They were indeed blessed personally for each of us. You could really see it. It's not possible to see the changes with the capsules, but it's the same. When Medium João traveled to other parts of the country, we would fill two big trucks with the prepared bottles. I would have to drive carefully on the rugged highways so the bottles would not be broken.

Sometimes we would run out of herbs and would need to prepare more during the night for the morning session. This often took place in makeshift tents and during all kinds of inclement weather. Medium João would stay up all night with us. He never left until the work was complete and he was satisfied that we all had a comfortable place to sleep. Often, at the break of dawn, none of us would have slept. Some of us would still be preparing the herbs, while others were beginning to prepare for the morning session. Medium João would make coffee and otherwise attend to us. I am devoted to this kind and generous man. I will be at his side until he passes and joins Dom Inácio and Dr. Augusto in the spiritual realms. But let's not talk about that. Medium João will be here for a long, long time.

7

TOOLS, MODALITIES, AND PRAYERS

I have never healed anyone. God heals. God and Faith.

—João Teixeira de Faria

THE SACRED TRIANGLE AT THE CASA

Upon entering the Main Hall of the Casa, one's gaze is drawn to the large wooden triangle mounted on the wall behind the stage. Visitors use the triangle as a spot to pray and connect with the Entities. Written prayers and photos are placed in the bottom portion of the triangle until it overflows. At that time, a medium removes the slips of paper and pictures and takes them to the Entity.

Historically, the triangle is one of the oldest spiritual symbols. The hexagram—a starlike figure formed by two overlapping triangles—is associated with protection and warding off negative energy. The symbol can be found in a number of faiths and cultures: in Judaism, the Star of David; in Kabbalism, the Serifah; in Hinduism, the Shatkona; and in Christianity and some pagan sects, the Seal of Solomon: where the triangles are representative of the union of opposites—the tip of the first triangle reaching toward

The triangle above has been blessed by the Entities for the reader. You may also copy this photograph of the triangle. Place your head upon the triangle and pray, in order to send your wishes to the Entities. You may write down your worries and requests on a slip of paper and place it on the base of the triangle as well. After a few days, remove the paper and burn it. As you watch the flames, focus your intention on releasing your troubles to the Divine. Then visualize the many blessings that are being sent to you.

heaven and the tip of the second grounded in the earthly plane. In a universal sense, the triangle symbolizes the transmutation brought forth by a union of components, such as the divine masculine and feminine. At the Casa, it is a symbol offered to help us focus so we can readily connect with the Divine. Viewed in this framework, the triangle is the aggregate of three principles that guide a proper spiritual life: love (tolerance, respect, and kindness to others), relief (caring for the community through good works), and truth (authentically being ourselves). As the Entity Dr. Valdivino has remarked, " The triangle symbolizes the sacred family, and the center is the ever-present One God."

HEALING

With every new day, we have opportunities to heal our illness or acquire more. Above all, the best medicine is a healthy will, because a feeble will weakens the imagination, and a feeble imagination weakens the body. A disease of the body can create disease of the soul, and disease of the soul can provoke a disease of the body.

—Andre Luiz, channeled by Chico Xavier

The Entities view the body as a hologram; they are able to see our energetic field and have access to our complete karmic history (the cumulative effects of all our actions). As we stand before the Entities and ask for healing, we must understand that we are entering into a partnership: we are co-creating healing by using our free will in a proactive way and making a concerted effort to change our lifestyle, habits, and anything else that no longer serves our highest good. Before going to the Casa, ask yourself what healing means to you. Carefully consider what your expectations are and what you are willing to contribute to your healing. Healing comes in many forms; sometimes we receive healing in unexpected ways or in ways not clear to us. It is important to remain as open as possible to the process, surrender our will, and have compassion for ourselves. Consider the following example of how the Entities work:

Karen had migraines and asked to be healed of her pain. She had suffered from cluster headaches since she was a little girl, vomiting in order to relieve the pain. The Entity (Dr. Augusto) told her that she would receive everything she asked for, but he did not give a timeline. On her second visit, a year later, she went before the Entity and again asked for help with her migraines. The Entity looked at her and said, "Yes, she is right. This filha has had headaches all her life. I am helping." He put his hand on her head and sent her to the current. She has never had another migraine headache since that day. During the time between these two visits, her headaches had become worse. She had several healing crises and took care of many issues in her life. Finally, she was ready to accept physical healing.

If you go before the Entities and ask them to "fix" you, they will try; however, they will also try to impart the awareness that "fixing" will not really resolve your karma. Each person's timeline for healing is different. Someone who has cancer might not have the luxury of waiting for a physical healing. Each person has free will.

Our physical well-being is distorted by beliefs, spirit-level karma, and karma that is stored in the body at a cellular level. Healing is the resolution of distortion so the physical body can receive a direct message from the Divine.

The following examples show the differences in healing that may be experienced at the Casa:

Someone is sick and all he knows is, "My belly hurts. I have a wife and five children. I cannot work my farm. They will starve! Heal me." The Entities do not enter into a higher level of healing. The concern is to release this man from this pain so he can get back to his life, work his farm, and support his family. They realize that this is not the end of pain in his life. He might mangle his hand in farm equipment or have a child die from sickness. The man is not seeking enlightenment at that point. He just wants his belly to stop hurting so he can work and feed his family.

Another man comes with the same belly pain and says, "Heal me!" This man has a deep spiritual practice. He sees the way he holds tension and anger in his belly. He understands that he needs a deeper healing. Here, the Entities may not work so quickly to heal the abdominal pain. It will depend on his karma. Pain is not necessary for learning. Paying attention is what is necessary.

The Entities will review this man's karma and his depth of understanding. They will work with his highest self to understand his deepest intention. They are never manipulative. They would not keep pain or distortion present in the body so that you have that nudge to pay attention. You are co-creating the healing with them. If you are truly willing to pay attention, so that your intention is to do both, to heal the body and to heal the deeper levels, this is what they will do, help to heal the body and continue to support the deepening work.[1]

The Entities and Medium João constantly remind us that healing works in conjunction with traditional medicine. They urge us to continue following our medical protocols and simply add the Passiflora capsules—not instead of, but as well as. The Entities will never tell us to stop taking our prescribed medicine. They remind us that Earth doctors are also messengers of God.

Occasionally, people come to the Casa in the final stages of an illness. Their organs are too depleted to hold the energy of a physical healing. This is not a failure, nor should it be seen as a judgment on the individual's willingness or ability to receive healing. Healing also takes place on the spiritual and karmic levels, and the soul often receives great support in preparing for transition. Many family members who lost a loved one after visiting John of God

---

1. Excerpted from a channeled session by author and teacher Barbara Brodsky.

have shared the person's feelings of serenity and equanimity and explained how the entire family shared in this healing. One such case involved a young woman who was ravaged by cancer and heavily dependent on morphine by the time she arrived at the Casa. She became dehydrated and was taken to the hospital, where she received an intravenous solution to replace the fluids and minerals in her body. She became stronger, and after a few days her pain completely disappeared. She returned to America in a serene state and absolute clarity of mind. Her family shared that her transition was peaceful and her family felt very supported.

Medium João suggests that an extremely ill person can be served best by sending a photograph to the Entities first, and they will say whether or not the person is strong enough to make the journey to the Casa. They will offer advice as to what healing protocols are in the person's best interest: herbs, blessed water, or perhaps surrogate surgery. Any one of these treatments offers substantive healing and the person will be told when they are strong enough to make the trip. Unfortunately, there are those instances when someone in the final stages of life makes the journey to the Casa with the intention of never returning home. These situations are precarious and often result in procedural and legal difficulties for the Casa and Medium João.

We are asked to take our healing seriously at the Casa, which includes drinking plenty of blessed water, taking ample time to rest, adhering to the dietary restrictions, partaking of the Casa soup, and not receiving any treatments from other healers during the forty days after surgery. Spiritual surgery offers powerful healing, and while you may not feel as if you had surgery, it is important to be vigilant and not overexert yourself: for example, walking to the waterfall instead of taking a taxi, lifting heavy objects, taking hikes or long walks. These actions often cause injury to internal sutures, which may not be visible on the body. This has been proven with X-rays and MRIs.

Heather shares a story about post-surgery:

I once gave four people the usual post-surgery recommendation to rest for twenty-four hours. I was surprised to see three of them walking in the field in front of the hotel later that afternoon. They said they felt no pain and were convinced they did not need to rest. I quickly ushered them back to bed, but by dinnertime they were all throwing up. They were convinced it was food poisoning. I wanted to be sure about the cause of their symptoms, so I asked the Entity for permission to bring these individuals before him. (We are advised not to return to the current rooms until at least twenty-four hours after surgery because the body's auric field is open, leaving an individual energetically vulnerable. This includes not returning to the Casa to go before the Entity.) The Entity pointed to three of them and said they were merely experiencing the effects of spiritual surgery; they were told to return to bed. The fourth person was told, "You will feel worse for four days, but you will leave here cured." It happened exactly as the Entity said. This person had come to the Casa with myasthenia gravis, and she has remained healthy and symptom-free ever since.

Carlos Appel, M.D., is a medium of the Casa and recently moved to Abadiânia from the south of Brazil. His daughter, Tânia, alternates between leading the first current and assisting in the surgery room. Dr. Carlos is a good friend of Medium João, and he generously serves the Casa and surrounding community as a medical doctor. We are very grateful to him for his service. He recently wrote this article:

The primary healing modality of the Casa de Dom Inácio de Loyola is the presence of Dom Inácio (St. Ignatius) and the other highly evolved spiritual Entities who assist in the transformation of denser energies into light. The capability for this is provided through the current of energy generated by participants meditating in the current rooms, bringing through a high level of vibratory frequencies, creating energy for use by these Entities. The current also sustains and provides strength and protection for John of God and his body/mind/spirit during the arduous process of incorporation. An important benefit is given to the meditating participants, as these higher frequencies transmute lower frequencies within their bodies.

It is a complicated procedure for most Entities to enter our low vibrational plane, and it entails an enormous expenditure of their energy for the treatment of our physical and spiritual ailments. Many "brothers and sisters" fail to appreciate the Entities' sacrifice and do not follow their advice, especially when it requires a change of lifestyle or deep personal transformation.

The healing properties of the herbal supplements, which are imbued with energy for each person individually, require a basic psychological and dietary environment to be effective. Some people find it difficult to change their lifestyles and their physical, emotional, or mental habits and to heed the spiritual advice they have received, but they still expect a miraculous healing. The healing cannot be received due to a lack of personal involvement in the healing process.

Sometimes the physical cure doesn't happen because the Entities' primary objective is different from our own; their primary focus for healing is within the realm of the immortal spirit. Their focus is in the elevation of the soul to bring about alignment and harmony with Divine Law. Sometimes a disease is necessary for the Spirit. The Law may find it consistent to keep the body weak to prevent more serious illness, which may lead to a continuing of the spiritual pain, or pain in future lives. Many enlightened people realize that pain and suffering can be the most effective medicine for spiritual recovery. We are responsible for our own health or disease, our joy or sadness. Each person must take charge of their own healing.[2]

CURRENT ROOM GUIDELINES

CLOTHING

As discussed previously, the Entities prefer that everyone who comes for healing wear white clothing in order to enhance visibility of the auric field.

KEEP EYES CLOSED

Always keep your eyes closed during the healing sessions, no matter which current room you sit in. This protocol allows the Entities to keep the chain of energy flowing.

ARMS AND LEGS

Keep your hands and feet uncrossed so the current will remain strong. This helps the Entities tap into the energy available for healings. When we cross our arms and legs in the current rooms, we keep the flow just for ourselves. We become a broken link in the chain. The current becomes weaker when even one person crosses their arms or legs, or opens their eyes. The Entities are sensitive to this phenomenon and the corresponding drop in the energy of the current.

HOLDING THE CURRENT

Author and worldwide shamanic teacher Sandra Ingerman lectures and teaches transmutation of environmental and personal toxins. The following excerpt from Sandra's book *Medicine for the Earth* is a powerful formula that we believe can be very helpful for holding the energy of the current:

2. Carlos Appel, M.D., Abadiânia, February 4, 2006.

To heal the Earth through transmutation, you must be willing to call forth your divinity and join together with your community to birth the holy, divine energy that transmutes your environment. The formulas for transmutation used here are: Intention, love, harmony, focus, union, concentration, and imagination.

Intention: You must have a clear intention to put aside your Egoic feelings of separation and use your spiritual energy to create healing and transformation in sacred space.

Love: You must love yourself, other people, and all living beings to invoke divine energy.

Harmony: You must harmonize your energy with your spiritual side and the spiritual energy of others.

Union: When you allow your spiritual energy to merge with the spiritual energy of others, you create the divine child. This third energy can create transmutation.

Focus: It takes focused intention to transform energy in a group.

Concentration: You must concentrate your efforts on holding your intention to bring love, harmony, and union into your environment.

Imagination: You must invoke your imagination to believe that you can really be a part of creating a healing space.[3]

THE WATERFALL

The Entity will often recommend a trip to the sacred waterfall as part of the healing treatment. All waterfalls are sacred, as is nature itself. Nature effortlessly reflects the highest truth of who we are.

3. Sandra Ingerman, *Medicine for the Earth* (New York: Three Rivers Press, 1994).

Poets remind us to seek refuge in nature, writing of its splendid beauty. Quiet waters, high mountaintops, and deep, lush forests once comforted humans. Now, because of high-speed communication and other technologies, humanity is inundated with images, sounds, and sights for our amusement and distraction that make us forget our innate and intimate connection to the elements.

The Casa waterfall, known as *Cachoeira de Lázaros*, is a half mile walk from the Casa. The waterfall itself is small, nestled at the end of a wooded, downhill path and flanked on either side by smooth gray stones. The waterfall is energized by the *Devas* (spirit beings) of nature and angels drawn to this area through the work of John of God. As you enter this sacred place, align yourself with the increased vibratory force and partake in a spiritual cleansing. A visit to the waterfall is an opportunity to refresh your body and your consciousness. The Entities ask that you follow a few simple guidelines:

▲ Only go to the waterfall with the permission of the Entities.

▲ Always go with someone. Limit your time to less than five minutes. Honor those waiting.

▲ Do not add candles, soap, or other objects to the falls or remove rocks or crystals.

▲ Respect this sanctuary and do not litter the environment.

▲ Male and females should go separately, preferably in groups.

▲ Wear a bathing suit. No photographs should be taken.

▲ Rest for forty-eight hours after surgery. Take a taxi to the waterfall until after your eight-day, post-surgery review.

▲ Please do not visit the waterfall after 5:00 P.M.

Heather relates:

I have seen snakes several times at the waterfall. I say this not to alarm you but to alert you. Let us be mindful that we share this space with all of nature. Be careful where you walk, stay on the pathways, and do not go there after dark. Bring a companion with you when visiting the waterfall.

Snakes are extraordinary creatures; they do not wish to harm us. They are a symbol of transformation. Like the snake, we yearn to slough off our old habits, our "thick skins," and embrace our inner light and live from a place of radiance. We can call upon the power of the snake to help us with this lifelong work.

Although we are specifically asked not to take photographs at the waterfall, on one occasion the Entity (Dr. Augusto) asked Karen to go there: "Take seven photos, no more, no less. There will be a gift for you." When Karen showed the pictures to the Entity, he pointed out the subtle presence of spirit in each photo. There is a vibrational frequency to all matter, and images can be a powerful tool for healing. The pictures in this book can help us connect not only to the divine resonance of the Casa but also to our spiritual light bodies. This creates a force field of healing energy that can help transform and uplift us.

CASA CRYSTAL TREATMENTS

The crystal bed is a healing modality that uses an array of specially cut and lighted quartz crystals. A session on the crystal bed is often prescribed by the Entities for rejuvenation, alignment, and in preparation for further healing work. These sessions help balance, clear, and restore the body's energetic template.

Crystal bed sessions last for twenty minutes. The person receiving the session rests face up with eyes closed as they bathe in the light energy of the crystals. The colored lights correspond to the seven chakras, which are energy centers that spin the energy through our energetic and meridian system. Light and color shine through each crystal in an alternating pattern, creating a spiraling amplification of vital energy. *Chakra* is a Sanskrit word for "wheel" and refers to the seven energy centers of the body. Chakras are aligned in an ascending center column from the base of the spine to the top of the head. The chakras spin and draw in the life force energy (Prana/Chi/Ki) to keep the physical and subtle bodies in balance. The *meridian system*, as described in Chinese medicine, is a network of energy pathways of the body's vital life force.

Crystals are capable of transmitting, storing, and modulating energy. The highly organized state of the quartz crystals allows photons to move without being trapped and condensed as in other forms of matter. A crystal is, therefore, a tool for using light and energy in specific ways. The health-giving effects of crystal therapy result from the vibration of the crystals resonating with the water in our tissues and cells. Structured water has increased surface tension and bonding properties. It is the pure state of water found in healthy cell tissue. Cancer cells and other unhealthy cells contain unstructured water. The vibrational patterns amplified by the Casa crystal bed treatments manifest as higher and higher levels of order, harmony, and awareness. Often the presence of the Entities can be felt during these treatments.

BLESSED WATER

Water is one of the primary elements that make up the body—approximately 70 percent of the human body is water, along with the elements of earth, fire, air, and ether. It fills our cells with life-giving Prana/Chi/Ki and nourishes us. Dehydration quickly takes our life force away, but we can be re-energized with pure water. Our blood is the inner stream that carries vital nutrients throughout the body and disposes of toxins. To quote Masaru Emoto in *The Secret Life of Water*, "Water has a memory and carries within it our thoughts and prayers. As you yourself are water, no matter where you are, your prayers will be carried to the rest of the world."

The Casa water has been energetically enhanced by the Entities to help us heal. We drink the blessed Casa water as part of our protocol while we are in Abadiânia and also at home. People undergo a powerful detoxification program while at the Casa, and dehydration is avoided by drinking two or more liters per day. The Entities often prescribe only water, not herbs. They have requested that the Casa water be poured into a glass, not drunk directly from the bottle. Should you visit the Casa or attend a program with John of God in another country, be sure to take some of this blessed water with you when you return home in order to continue and strengthen the healing process.

The Casa has received many testimonials regarding the dramatic healing effect of Casa water. For example, one woman came to the Casa to ask for help for her father, who was receiving last rites in the hospital. The Entity told her to take a bottle of Casa water and drive straight to the hospital. She was to put the Casa water on his eyelids and lips. The next day, her father recovered and is still alive, eight years later.

Kathy Clifford arrived in July 2005, emaciated and in agony from bone cancer. She even brought her own special trampoline bed to sleep on. She was given some cotton wool and a bottle of Casa water, and it was suggested that her friend, Margaret, swab her spine with the water while visualizing it as liquid light. Her pain was immediately alleviated and she slept well. Kathy continued to use this treatment every night while she was in Brazil. When she returned later that year, she had put on eight pounds and no longer needed her special bed. Chapter 10 includes a more detailed story about Kathy Clifford's healing experiences with John of God.

Another woman, who had undergone extensive medical surgery in the United States, treated one-half of her large scar and bruising with Casa water. She did not treat the other half with the water. There was an astounding difference in her healing process. The treated area healed almost immediately, but the untreated scar and bruise took much longer.

MEDIUMSHIP AT THE CASA

We are all inherently mediums, but occasionally the Entity declares someone to be an official "Medium of the Casa." He asks that the person's name be registered at the Casa office, and an identity card is created and then signed by Medium João. This recognition also brings deeper responsibilities of service, some of which are listed below:

1. Become acquainted with and diligently follow the Rules of the Casa, and inform others.

2. Kindly assist those who come to the Casa. Always practice charity and communicate to all with love, compassion, respect, forgiveness, humility, and kindness. Remember that when you engage in these practices you are creating a peaceful and harmonious environment for all.

3. Observe the rule of silence in the Great Hall and current rooms during Casa sessions.

4. Assist, whenever necessary, during Casa sessions by helping to form single, orderly lines in the Great Hall and reminding visitors to maintain silence, keep their eyes closed, and uncross their arms and legs.

5. Diligently observe Casa current room hours: 7:45 A.M. and 1:45 P.M. Always enter from the first current room, not the surgery room. Arrive on time and attend the opening prayers. Help inform others as to the current session times.

6. Enter into a single-file line at the current room door in silence. Give preference to the handicapped.

7. Expand your intellectual and spiritual evolution by reading the writings of Chico Xavier and Allan Kardec as well as the Casa books.

8. Assist in taking people to the waterfall and observe waterfall codes of behavior.

9. Avoid disturbing Medium João by going to his office excessively for consultations in between Casa sessions. It is important to honor and respect his privacy, remembering it

is essential for Medium João's health and well-being to rest during these intervals.

PRAYERS

Upon arising, thank God for the blessing of life. If you are not in the habit of praying, be composed and recall old thoughts of serenity and optimism for a few moments before resuming activity.

—The Entity Andre Luiz, channeled by Chico Xavier

Medium João's favorite prayer is the Prayer of Caritas. He always begins the healing sessions by speaking the first lines of this prayer and continuing until he incorporates. We offer here the Prayer of Caritas in its entirety, an ancient Aramaic version of the Lord's Prayer, as it was written before it was translated into Greek and Latin, and the Divine Mother's Prayer.

THE PRAYER OF CARITAS

God. Our Father, who hath the power and the goodness, give strength to those who suffer privation, give light to those who seek the truth, put compassion and charity into the hearts of mankind.

God. Give the traveler a guiding star, consolation to the anxious, and rest to the sick.

Father. Give repentance to the guilty, truth to the spirit, a guide for the children, and a father to the orphans.

Lord. May your goodness blanket everything you have created.

Piety, Lord, to those who know you not, hope to those who suffer. May your goodness allow the consoling spirits to spread peace, hope, and faith all over.

God. A ray of light, a spark of your love can scorch the earth. Allow us to drink from the fountain of your fertile and infinite goodness, and all tears will dry, all pain will subside, and only heart and thought will rise up to you as a cry of recognition and of love.

As Moses on the mountain, we await you with open arms. Oh Power. Oh Goodness. Oh Beauty. Oh Perfection. We want somehow to achieve your mercy.

God. Give us the strength to help our progress, enabling us to rise up to you. Give us pure charity. Give us faith and reason. Give us the humbleness that will make of our souls a mirror to reflect your image.

Amen.[4]

THE LORD'S PRAYER

(*Directly translated from the Aramaic into English, rather than from Aramaic to Greek, to Latin, to old English, to modern English*)

O cosmic Birther of all radiance and vibration. Soften the ground of our being and carve out a space within us where your presence can abide.

Fill us with your creativity so that we may be empowered to bear the fruit of your mission.

Let each of our actions bear fruit in accordance with our desire.

Endow us with the wisdom to produce and share what each being needs to grow and flourish.

Untie the tangled threads of destiny that bind us, as we release others from the entanglement of past mistakes.

Do not let us be seduced by that which would divert us from our true purpose, but illuminate the opportunities of the present moment.

4. Psychographed Christmas Night, 1873, by Mme. W. Krell in Bordeaux, France, from the spirit entity Caridade (Caritas, or Charity). Reference: *The Casa Prayer Book*, Casa de Dom Inácio, Abadiânia, Brazil.

For you are the ground and the fruitful vision, the birth, power, and fulfillment, as all is gathered and made whole once again.

Amen.

THE DIVINE MOTHER'S PRAYER

Our Mother, whose body is the Earth,

Sacred is thy being. Thy gardens grow

Thy will be done in our cities, as it is in nature.

Thanks be this day for food, air, and water.

Forgive us our sins against the Earth, as we are learning to forgive one another.

And surrender us not into extinction, but deliver us from our folly.

For thine is the beauty and the power, and all life, from birth to death,

From beginning to end. Amen.

So be it forever. Blessed be.

POST-SURGERY GUIDELINES

The Casa protocols are updated regularly. Please check with Casa staff or your tour guide for additional instructions.

DIETARY RESTRICTIONS

After surgery and when taking herbs, please follow these dietary guidelines: abstain from chili peppers, alcohol, pork, and anything containing pork, including bacon, ham, salami, sausage, and soups such as split pea with ham.

SEXUAL ACTIVITY AND EXERCISE

A forty-day rest period is needed after surgery. Strenuous exercise such as running, yoga, power walking, or weightlifting should be avoided. Abstinence from sexual intercourse for forty days after the first surgery and eight days after all subsequent surgeries is required. Our bodies need this vital energy in order to heal. Any strenuous movement could interfere with deep surgery and perhaps undo internal sutures.

SPIRIT ATTACHMENT AND POSSESSION

The phenomena of spirit attachment and possession of humans by unevolved, discarnate spirits is a common occurrence dealt with at the Casa, although most people are unaware and unaffected by this. These spirits are so attached to the earthly plane that they are unaware they have left their bodies. The Entities lovingly and compassionately free them so they can go to the place where they belong in the spirit world. Guided by a team of Entities, specially trained mediums (known as *transport mediums*) work in the current rooms and assist in this endeavor.

This type of cleansing also heals the person to whom the confused spirit was attached. One of the reasons it is so important to keep our eyes closed in the current rooms when we are meditating is to add to our protection and to assist the inner work that is constantly being done for the benefit of the living and the discarnate. It is always important to pray and free ourselves from negative emotions. This strengthens our energy field. Confused, discarnate spirits have no interest in the auric field of a positive, loving, and happy person—just as an infection cannot penetrate our immune system when it is healthy and strong. There is a veil of protection over the Casa and the entire area that keeps everyone safe from these lower vibrations and spirit attachments.

LEAVING THE CASA

Many people leave for home on Fridays, and there is a great deal of pressure to receive everyone before their departure. Medium João's body is tired, and the Entities want the afternoon session to proceed as smoothly as possible. The Entity sometimes becomes upset and says, "This person was seen this morning; there is no need to come by again. They are being treated in the current."

At the end of the session, listen for the invitation by the leader of the current room to say farewell to the Entity and receive any suggested herbal prescriptions. This invitation is *only* for people who did *not* pass before the Entity that morning. Please stay seated until you are called to form a line. The flow of the current is broken when everyone gets up at the same time. Always move quietly and carefully. If you passed before the Entity in the morning, you can use this time to offer prayers of gratitude. Visualize a clearing and cleansing for yourself and the other people in the room before departing. The Entity will choose one or two mediums to do the closing prayer. They will ask us to participate in a prayer of spiritual cleansing for the world, for Abadiânia, for the Casa, and for each person gathered that day. The closing prayer is for our continued protection and healing.

8

TRIPS ABROAD

Why do they not invite me to the hospitals? I could help them there as well.

—Dr. Oswaldo Cruz, April 2006

Medium João has traveled to many countries. The Entities have asked him to do this work and, ever faithful to his commitment, he travels wherever the guiding spirits lead him. These brief but intense trips, when he sees thousands of people a day, weigh heavily upon Medium João. His body is strong but the work is physically exhausting, and he demands a great deal of himself in his service to humanity. He shows immense dedication to his mission, and at the same time we are reminded of his humanity.

All said and done, Medium João is Brazilian. He has fun wherever he goes. He does a little sightseeing, but he does not want special attention. He is constantly concerned with the welfare of his staff, making sure everyone is comfortable and well cared for. He prefers to stay in his hotel room, and often he will gather a few intimate friends around in the evening to eat, talk, laugh, and tell stories. Sometimes he puts on music and dances the samba. He loves innocent pranks, but his humor is never malicious or offensive. One day, after seeing over three thousand people in Germany,

Medium João told marvelous stories of his childhood. He finds it difficult to sleep at night after the long sessions and is often awake until dawn. As previously mentioned, he works spiritually around 2:00 A.M., and these commitments often take many hours.

While working in other places, the Entity will often say to people, "I want to see you in Brazil" or "For your work, I need to see you in Brazil." Although the current can be set up anywhere, temporary currents do not carry the same potency as in Abadiânia. Medium João is freer to do physical surgeries in Brazil, and people receive a deeper transmission of spiritual energy there. The Casa current creates a powerful force field formed by the concentration of the experienced Casa mediums. This potent energy field is based upon a greater foundation: the energy that emanates from the land itself. In Abadiânia, as in so many sacred sites, there is an energy vortex that supports the spiritual work. When the Entities suggest a person visit the Casa for deeper healing, it is because they need to experience this energy field.

Although Medium João does not talk about it, the incorporation of the Entities in different places around the world is necessary because of the transition humanity is going through. He is a vessel for spreading the light of consciousness around the Earth. Each hand that he touches, each glance that he gives, carries this accelerated infusion of light, altruism, and grace. Like a source candle, those who are touched carry this light wherever they go and multiply the light with everyone they meet.

THE PHALANGE IN PERU

One day in 2005, while working in the current room, Heather was concerned about obtaining the facts for this book, in particular, about Medium João and his trip to Peru. The Entity (Dr. Valdivino) called her over to him and said, "Filha, go to the Casa store and buy the book by Liberato Povoa. He was with Medium João in Peru. There you will find the answers to your questions. You can use that book." Heather bought the recommended book, and while reading it she felt the energy of the Entities' coming through the written word. Judge Povoa is a prolific legal writer and a high court judge. As a frequent visitor to the Casa and a medium, he is a close friend and confidant of Medium João.

Medium João went to Lima, Peru, for the first time in 1991. He was sponsored by government official Luis Rosello, who had visited the Casa and been cured of a heart condition. Medium João took a large committee of mediums, lawyers, and nurses with him. The Medical Association of Peru was threatened by Medium João and his abilities as a healer, and they managed to get him arrested and jailed. Many people had already been healed and responded with mass protests. Medical doctors vouched for his authenticity, and Medium João was promptly released.

It is reported that over twenty thousand people were healed on this visit. The great majority of those seeking healing were afflicted with cholera because there was an epidemic at that time. During this trip, the Entities were visited by President Fujimori, who was healed of a muscular problem in his hands. His son was cured of a mental disturbance. Medium João was awarded the Medal of Honor by the Peruvian government.

Liberato Povoa was invited by Medium João to accompany him on his next mission to Peru, in 1994. His book, *João de Deus, Fenomeno de Abadiânia*, is beautifully written in Portuguese, and we would like to honor Judge Povoa by quoting and translating directly from it with regard to Medium João's memorable visit to Peru:

On January 18, 1994, we disembarked at dawn at the Lima International Airport. There was an absolute multitude of people already present. They were chanting and shouting Medium João's name. The police had come to cordon off the area to contain the crowds. Medium João was swarmed by TV, newspaper, and radio reporters.

We were in transit to our next destination, where the president of the Casa de Dom Inácio of Puno awaited us. Our flight landed briefly in Arequipa. We were not allowed to disembark, but from the airplane windows we could clearly see the multitude of people crowded in the confines of the airport courtyard. They were hoping for even a glimpse of the famous healer. We landed in Julaica, since there is no airport in Puno. The welcoming committee was waiting for us, because the terrorist group *Sendero Luminoso* was very active in the area. We were given very tight security. To give you an idea of the importance of Medium João's visit to Peru, the authorities of Puno had been allocated one hundred troops from an elite military unit commanded by several officers and two generals: Luiz Paz Cardenas and Luciano Cesar Ramirez Vinatea. This entourage protected us twenty-four hours a day, not only from the terrorist group, but also from being overwhelmed by the sea of people desperate to be blessed and reaching for even a piece of his clothing or anything they could hold on to as a relic. The organizers had prepared the *Clube de Tiro de Puno*, a large shooting range and country club, for the Entities to attend to the people.

Over the five days, he tended to 20,000 people. He performed over one thousand surgeries, physical and spiritual. On his previous trip to Peru, there had been resistance by the medical authorities. On this trip, he took several precautions, insisting on the presence of medical professionals and local government ministers to witness the operations. In Puno, there was a permanent presence of doctors, military and civilian, to witness the spiritual work.

There were also supervisors from the medical college as well as representatives from the prosecutor's office of Puno. The sessions commenced at 8:00 A.M. and continued until late at night, when we returned to the hotel. However, his work was never limited to this schedule. By 6:00 A.M., hundreds of people were already lined up waiting patiently outside of the hotel. The same was true when we returned in the evening. We would find a multitude waiting behind the security lines. Medium João insisted on tending to each person, one by one. If we were lucky, we would get to our rest by 2:00 A.M. We were exhausted at the end of the day, since there was only Doctora Neidi and me to translate from Spanish into Portuguese, thus requiring us to be at the side of the Entities throughout the trip.

We found ourselves struggling with the high altitude. Puno is 3,800 meters above sea level, with a population of 400,000. Our hotel was situated on Lake Titicaca, and we were given tea made from coca leaves as a remedy for altitude sickness. The air was so thin it was difficult to breathe. On opening the windows at night, the powerful energies and gentle breezes from the lake renewed us.

I was amazed by Medium João's stamina. Before going to work, he limited himself to one glass of papaya juice, not eating again until late at night. He ate nothing during incorporation. After attending to the people at the hotel, he would begin to work with the public waiting for him at the club. Men, women, and children, the elderly, crippled, and blind, and those stricken with a variety of illnesses spent all day waiting in single file in the cutting 8 degrees Celsius (46 degrees Fahrenheit) weather. Many had already spent two nights sleeping in the lines under these freezing and sometimes rainy conditions. It was a shocking contrast to notice the well-dressed people of means in line with the impoverished, the poor wearing only thin cotton *zorba* pants and shirts. Medium João's sense of justice does not permit privileges, and he insists that rich and poor wait together without favoritism. I have never experienced a more hospitable people. The Peruvian people have a singular education with innate wisdom. Even the children who could barely talk had a loving gesture or word for us. During the long lines, we bought candies and chocolate to distribute to the children, who were insufficiently clothed for the cold. Many mothers carried their children on their backs, as is the custom of indigenous people. On receiving our simple gifts, it was moving for us to see profound gratitude shining in their eyes followed by a captivating, "Gracias, Senhor."

To give you an idea of the enormity of the crowds, not one bottle of water remained in Puno to be blessed by the Entities. By the last day, we could see people carrying plastic bags containing both clear rainwater and, more often than not, muddy river water. We were extremely concerned because Peru is known for outbreaks of cholera. Puno has open sewers. It is a miracle that there was not one outbreak of cholera during Medium João's second mission in Peru. Finally, trucks brought in bottled water from the closest town, which was 350 miles away. Medium João does not allow his name to be commercialized, ever, and he refused endorsements from water companies during his trip to Peru.

Media coverage stimulated caravans of people from other Peruvian towns, as well as from Bolivia, Chile, and Venezuela, to come to Puno. Journalists from neighboring countries came in droves hoping to interview the Brazilian medium.

Under the vigilant watch of members of the public ministry and medical profession of Peru, hundreds of physical operations were carried out for a plethora of illnesses. Some of the doctors and public officials even voluntarily submitted to surgery.

Countless extraordinary healings took place, including a young girl about fourteen years of age, who was a folklore dancer from Cusco. Having suffered a car accident, she was now reduced to walking with crutches. The Entity massaged both her legs and then ordered, "Walk. You are healed." Before the incredulous eyes of hundreds, he dramatically threw her crutches down onto the ground with a resounding crash. The girl, initially with difficulty, began to walk supported only by the roaring applause of the crowd. Later on, we saw her walking almost normally, still weeping in gratitude and surrounded by her family.

There were many such cases of crutches being thrown to the ground. The public applause alerted TV crews and journalists, who would run to the scene. Many were unable to contain their own emotions while interviewing the person who had been healed. During one morning session alone, at the special request of General Cardenas, commander of the military in Puno, nearly a thousand military personnel and their family members were attended by the Entities.

Out of this group came a young boy who had been afflicted with a crippling disease and who now walked with great difficulty, fully dependent on crutches. The Entity ordered him to walk. Few believed that this was possible, because they knew the boy had been treated by the top physical therapists and orthopedists without results. This was a high-profile family of the region and his case was well publicized. The crutches were taken from him and the crippled boy began to walk. The crowd was stunned by witnessing this miracle. The normally stoic General Paz could no longer hide his tears.

An old man arrived. According to family members who accompanied him, he had been completely deaf in both ears for many years. The Entity put his palms over the old man's ears. After a few moments, he questioned the family, "What is his name?" Upon being told his name was *Vicente*, the Entity directed somebody to step back two or three meters from the deaf man and address him in a normal tone of voice. The family members, knowing he was stone deaf, looked at each other doubtfully. When he was called by his name, Vicente turned toward the voice. Immediately, someone else spoke his name and he turned around to face that person. He could hear everything that was said to him. The man and his family left in a flood of tears, giving their interviews to the media.

Later that day, a woman appeared before the Entity with her twelve-year-old son. She was sobbing from gratitude. She told us that her son had suffered from insanity since birth. Oftentimes, he required physical restraints and was unable to lead a normal life. Even special schooling or private tutoring was out of the question because of the gravity of his mental derangement. On Medium João's previous trip to Peru, not only had President Fujimori and his son been cured, but evidently this young boy had also been cured of his insanity. This time, his mother had spent two days standing in line with her son under the freezing conditions and drizzling rain, not to request further healing, but to present her moving testimony and thank the Entity for curing her son. In his own clear voice, the young boy told us he was studying in Lima at a regular school and progressing remarkably well in his studies.

Commander Mario Garcia Noe of the national Peruvian police had been a victim of a terrorist attack. He had received a spinal injury that reduced him to a paraplegic. He was completely paralyzed from the waist down. He received energy from the Entity and sat in the current throughout all the sessions. On the last day, as we departed for Lima, Commander Mario was already able to stand up from his wheelchair. Still needing support, he had been given hope of rehabilitation, should he choose to come to Brazil and continue his treatment.

Before leaving Puno, Medium João was honored by a military unit of the state in which Puno is located. The military marched past him in their full dress uniforms, honoring and saluting him in the pouring rain. This military tribute is usually reserved for respected heads of state.

JOHN OF GOD VISITS ATLANTA, GEORGIA

People from around the country and the world converged on Atlanta, Georgia, in the spring of 2006. A collective cry for help was heard in the spirit realms, as the sick, the wheelchair-bound, the troubled, and the lonely flowed into the large conference center.

John of God finished his work at the Casa in Brazil at 6:00 P.M. on Friday, the night before he was due to leave for Atlanta. His wife, Ana, had arranged their flight so they could arrive in a timely fashion on Saturday, the day before the first session. John of God works tirelessly in his mission, and although his body can be exhausted by the hours he keeps, he loves his work and was excited to be with the approximately 2,500 Americans who were coming to see him and the Entities.

After they arrived in Atlanta, he rested while waiting for Heather to accompany him to meet the volunteers, become acquainted with the premises, and set the foundation for the work the following day. Throughout the three days Medium João was in Atlanta, Heather served as his personal attendant and translator. She also translated for the Entities during the sessions.

The lobby was a sea of white each morning of the three-day event. The volunteers instructed the people who were waiting to form a line and then ushered them into the temporary "Great

Hall." John of God came in and thanked everyone, including the American authorities, for allowing him to be in Atlanta. Then he turned to go through the curtains and into his current room. Holding Heather's hand, he left his body and incorporated an Entity. One by one, the thousands of "children" were seen. Some came reverently; others were skeptical. Some people did not know what to expect and seemed confused as they filed past the Entity. They did not understand how their healing could start with only a brief glance and a wave of his hand, saying, "I will do your work," or "Come to Brazil and I will finish your work." Many people felt the ever-present energy of the current, and it gave them faith that such a small window in time was simultaneously an infinite moment in other dimensions, where the cure for their ailment or problem had already begun.

At one point, the Entity took a woman's cane away from her and threw it on the floor, telling her to walk. She continues to do well without her cane. Divine love healed the people and tears flowed spontaneously from many, as the emotions of gratitude could no longer be contained. Their faith in God began to be restored and their doubts started to dissolve. The greatest healing, the healing of spirit, was given to those who wished to receive it.

While in Atlanta, John Quinones from *Prime Time Live* filmed an interview with João. The Entity spoke gently and kindly, reassuring Mr. Quinones of *his* connection to God. When asked why he came to America, and particularly Atlanta, the Entity replied that he came because there was so much faith here. He came because of love, and he was grateful that so many people had left their homes and made the journey to see him.

Medium João told Quinones, "I am here not to fool anyone. I am here because God is here. We are here to receive the energy of God, the Breath of God. I do not have a religion, but I believe in faith and the Universal God, which is Love. Everyone who has faith and has a religion is my brother, for we all believe in the One God, who is our Father. I do not preach a religion, but I uphold Universal Love and belief in the Creator of the Cosmos."

When asked why some people are healed and others are not, the Entity replied, "I am here to heal, but only God gives life."

During the lunch breaks and in the evening, John of God and his wife relaxed and visited with friends. Sometimes, he would lie back on the couch in the living area of his hotel room and fall asleep. He enjoys watching television, preferably Western movies. After the morning session, he would rest for an hour or two and then have a light lunch after making sure his staff had plenty to eat. Then he would take another short rest as he prepared himself for the work ahead.

The last day of the sessions in Atlanta closed at 5:30 P.M. on a Tuesday. John of God left for Brazil immediately, not wanting to miss a day of service to his community in Abadiânia. He left Atlanta at 8:00 P.M. on Tuesday night, and on Wednesday at 2:00 P.M. he was back at work incorporating the Entities in Abadiânia.

The Entities who announced themselves in Atlanta were Dr. José Valdivino, St. Francis Xavier, and Dr. Oswaldo Cruz, who asked if there were any medical doctors who wished to talk to him. Dr. Cruz was a brilliant bacteriologist. He graduated medical school at nineteen years of age and studied at the Pasteur Institute in Paris. The Entity then spoke with some of the medical doctors who approached. (See chapter 9 for more information about Dr. Cruz.)

Linda Hamilton, one of the participants in the Atlanta event, relates her experience:
I developed arthritis of the hip about the time my daughter was born in 1996. It grew progressively worse and I began to walk with a cane about two years ago. Before my arthritis, I was a high school gymnast, a dancer, and a figure-skating enthusiast.

I went to see John of God in Atlanta with my friend Anne. I met her last July at the Casa when we both went on a healing quest with Heather. I was frightened the first time I went before the Entity at the Casa. I had heard that he sometimes performs miraculous healings before the crowd. I didn't want this done to me. Something in me still resisted healing, but I loved the experience of going to the Casa and was hopeful that I would be healed.

I was in a different state of mind in Atlanta. Six months of herbs and invisible surgery were working on my soul and improving my approach on life. I had much more energy after the first Casa visit, but I still had pain, inflammation, and a lot of stiffness in my left hip and knee. I still needed my cane.

Two weeks before I left for Atlanta, I had a visit in the middle of the night. Around 2:00 A.M., I awoke from sleep knowing that someone nonphysical was with me. I wasn't dreaming. I was a little alarmed, but I knew the visitors were the Entities, although I thought at the time it was João. They asked me to keep my eyes closed as they worked on me, entering my body from my right hip. After this experience, I began to focus more of my mental and emotional energy on Atlanta and on my healing. I told Anne that the Entities were already in the United States to prepare us for the event.

We drove to Atlanta, where we met my eighty-year-old mother, who had agreed to come with us to meet Medium João. She couldn't travel to Brazil, but she could come to Georgia, where she had been born. I was so pleased she was going and knew it would make a difference for our entire family.

Anne was in front of me when I went before the Entity, and my mother was behind me. I saw Heather interpreting for him. I felt such love and gratitude for Medium João, the Entities, Heather, and the other Casa guides because they give so much. I felt extreme tenderness toward the Entity. I whispered "Friend of God" to him silently. I felt he was a Friend of God. I was a Friend of God. And God is our Friend. That point of view made all the difference. I could, and did, meet God's eyes. I loved him with all my heart. In return, he looked back at me and spoke with compassion and love, saying, "Do you really need this cane?"

Then I understood that I did not need it, and I obeyed the will of God. "I will put the cane away," I said.

The Entity took my cane and asked the people sitting in current and those in line, including my mother, to open their eyes and see the miracle of God at work. He told me to walk around the room. I walked like a lobster, in a lurching, lopsided manner, but I walked without pain. I was in a daze, not fully comprehending what was going on. I felt like I was being reborn, coming out before the world anew. It was my moment.

The Entity asked me to go and sit in current. Moments later, another man came in, having also lost his cane to God. My mother and Anne went on to receive invisible surgery or a blessing.

I never went before the Entities in Atlanta again. I was exhausted and excited. My leg sometimes hurt so badly that I didn't want to walk. At other times, I was strong enough to walk without the cane. Since returning home, I have been renovating my house and packing up a household to move, often by myself. I still rely on my cane about half of the time, but often I go without it, especially while doing the renovation work. I have faith that I will recover completely because God is my Friend and I am a Friend of God. I look forward to visiting the Entities and John of God again, and I thank him for his sacrifices on behalf of humankind. Because of him, I know God is at work in the world today.

9

SPIRITISM AND THE ENTITIES

*To be a medium requires loving God above all else. Love your fellow beings
as yourself. It is necessary to have a deep faith in a higher power.*

—John of God

Em Nome de Deus! (In the name of God!) Medium João's voice
resounded as he walked into the current room. Hundreds of
people from all parts of the globe had gathered in preparation for
the healing work of the day.

They sat quietly in meditation with their eyes closed. With a
jolt, Medium João left his body and an Entity incorporated. The
consciousness of John of God, the man, would now rest in a state
similar to sleep until the day's healing was complete.

Just who, or what, are the Entities that are so central to the
spiritual mission of Medium João? The spiritual work done at the
Casa is based on the principles of Spiritism: a doctrine that carefully examines the relationship between physical and nonphysical
realities. Physical beings constitute the visible or incarnate world,
while nonphysical beings constitute the spirit world. Viewed in
this framework, the Entities are highly evolved, discarnate spirits
who reach down from the spiritual world to relieve suffering. This

mission is facilitated through Medium João's willingness to offer his body as a vessel for this work.

There is a spiritual hierarchy at the Casa de Dom Inácio. Divine consciousness is the overarching force that guides all work. Next is the Entity known as *King Solomon*, and then St. Ignatius and his group consciousness, referred to as his "phalange of spirits." Then there are the Entities who were physicians in prior incarnations: Drs. Augusto de Almeida, Oswaldo Cruz, and José Valdivino. There are those nameless Entities who remark, *"Salve (hail) Dr. Augusto"* as they incorporate. They are either in his phalange, or perhaps Dr. Augusto serves as their mentor. Others share little or nothing about themselves yet offer a great deal of love, guidance, and kindness. One such Entity says his name is "José" and another "Love." Still another states he is not worthy to kneel at the feet of St. Ignatius. This Entity, identifying himself as a member of St. Ignatius's phalange, reminds us that people who visit the Casa are most fortunate because they are able to be with St. Ignatius when he incorporates through Medium João. And while the mission of these discarnate spirits is to offer us healing, it is important to remember that their efforts contribute to their own advancement in the spiritual realms.

Following are short descriptions of the more well known Entities who work at the Casa.

ST. IGNATIUS OF LOYOLA (1491–1556)

It has been said that St. Ignatius of Loyola (also known as *Dom Inácio*) is an improbable saint, one who we can easily relate to: a man who lived life with great zeal and took great pleasure in the pursuit of fine women, food, and drink.

Historians have written that he was a rather attractive and vain man, immensely stubborn, with a fierce temper and a heightened sense of entitlement. And yet this man, filled at times with self-hatred and fear that God could not love him because of his sins, came to know God's love and mercy. A new life of humility, poverty, and charity filled him with peace. The latter part of his life was devoted to inspiring others to seriously concern themselves with their spiritual growth.

Iñigo de Oñaz y Loyola was born in 1491, into a family of Basque nobility, the youngest of thirteen children. He spent much of his youth with wealthy relatives in the court of King Ferdinand of Spain, where he acquired a taste for the finer things in life. After Ferdinand's death, Iñigo enlisted in the Spanish army. In 1521, when French troops invaded the town of Pamplona, Iñigo and his compatriots engaged in a fierce battle to reclaim the city. While defending the Pamplona fortress he was gravely wounded and his leg was shattered by artillery.

Vanity drove Iñigo to endure several painful surgeries in the hope of re-shaping his deformed leg, but it never properly healed, leaving him with a limp for the remainder of his life. (When St. Ignatius incorporates, Medium João walks with a discernable limp.) His convalescence was long and painful, and Iñigo sought refuge in books. Once he had read everything in the family library, he was left with two choices: a book on the life of Christ and another on the lives of saints. Stories of hardship, piety, and service to God inspired Iñigo to re-evaluate his life; daydreams of heroism and chivalry left him bitter, empty, and depressed. Regret and remorse filled Iñigo's soul, and in 1522 he traveled to the sacred shrine of the Black Madonna in Montserrat. This sojourn was different from the many before, made by a valiant knight seeking blessings and protection for future battles. At the altar of the Madonna, Iñigo laid down his sword and shield, confessed his sins, and headed off to Manresa. Thus began Iñigo's own experience of living a spiritual life: begging for alms, going without food, engaging in constant prayer, and harsh penance practices.

Iñigo seized this opportunity to deepen his education, traveling throughout Spain and then France, immersing himself in the classic works of the period. He attended college in Paris, received a degree in fine arts, and took a new name: *Ignatius of Loyola*. Throughout his travels, he took every opportunity to share with others his spiritual experiences and was often imprisoned for his beliefs. Yet he continued to persevere, enduring hardships and illness, and holding a steadfast belief in God's divine plan for humanity. The last years of his life were spent educating others, a quest that resulted in the founding of the order known as the Society of Jesus in 1540. He continued with his mission of tending to the spiritual and material needs of the poor until his death in 1556.

Ignatius wrote several treatises throughout his lifetime, drawing upon his own personal spiritual struggles. The treatise *The Spiritual Exercises of Saint Ignatius* was born out of his desire to write a manual of directives for those who wish to align their lives with God. In it, Ignatius offers a precise formula of prayers, confessions, and meditations for spiritual inquiry and growth over a four-week period. And yet at the Casa, during a three-day period each week, one finds the basic premise of Ignatius's treatise hard at work, as we offer ourselves to the Divine through meditation and prayer for spiritual inquiry and growth. Ignatius, the patron saint of the Casa de Dom Inácio advised that

> *The more we unite ourselves to Him (our Lord), the more do we dispose ourselves to receive graces and gifts from his divine and supreme goodness.*[1]

ST. IGNATIUS AT THE CASA

St. Ignatius always incorporates on the anniversary of his death. His energy is so strong that he limits his presence to twenty minutes, so as not to overly stress Medium João's body with high-frequency vibrations. Medium João's body seems quite different with the incorporation of St. Ignatius. It appears as if the vast and expansive high vibration of the Entity is being compressed into the

---

1. Saint Ignatius of Loyola, *The Spiritual Exercises of Saint Ignatius*, 29.

upper torso of Medium João's body, which struggles as if to find space to contain so much light and energy.

During incorporation on July 31, 2005, St. Ignatius fell to his knees in front of the Entity's chair as an energy wave visibly pulsated through everyone surrounding him. He looked heavenward and said, "I am being raised to another level." Medium João's body shuddered as St. Ignatius left and Dr. Augusto came through. He announced that the vibration of St. Ignatius has become so elevated that it would be difficult for any medium on Earth to incorporate the spirit of St. Ignatius. Dr. Augusto then handed a rose to one of the Casa mediums, who had come to the Casa after being told by her oncologist that her cancer was inoperable. Dr. Augusto said that every year during the celebration of St. Ignatius's feast day, he offers her a rose in commemoration of another year of life. Now, before all those present, Dr. Augusto asked her how many roses she had received. Sobbing, she said this was her eighth rose.

On Friday, July 28, 2006, the Casa celebrated the feast day of St. Ignatius.[2] Many months had been spent planning for the festivities of this auspicious day, as Casa volunteers diligently prepared for the busloads of Brazilians and throngs of foreigners who come to venerate the patron saint of the Casa.

The morning's incorporation seemed to take longer than usual. The mediums stood silent, focusing their energies on holding the space and offering prayers of thanks for the Entity's presence. As the spirit of St. Ignatius entered Medium João, Heather noted the physical change in João's appearance: his glasses had been removed and his hair pulled forward in front of his eyes. There was also a noticeable difference in the texture of his hair: a high gloss shine resulting from the energetic shift in the Medium's body. Now fully incorporated, the Entity spoke, *"I am the one who dragged my foot."* St.

---

2. The actual birthday is July 31, but the celebration is observed on a day when the Casa is in session.

Ignatius silently hugged those who approached, as is the usual custom for this day. As people opened their arms to be embraced they were in awe of the vast energy that radiated from João's body. The incorporation lasted about ten minutes. Then Dr. Augusto incorporated, sat in the Entity's chair, and spoke the following words:

> Dom Inácio is the light that comes through. Faith and concentration moves the energy to bring through the light. Dom Inácio oversees all the surgeries that take place at the Casa. He oversees and protects everything. You (indicating all those present) make a circle of concentration through current that brings in the light for the practice of good. To make a circle of light for the practice of good is easy.

And with that said and noted, the day of healing and celebration continued.

ST. FRANCIS XAVIER (1506–1552)

St. Francis Xavier is often referred to as the Apostle of the Indies and Japan. A devout man, dedicated to the salvation of souls, he spent his entire life traveling to distant lands spreading the word of God. Historians attribute Xavier's missionary success to his extraordinary negotiating skills; he was said to possess a gentle manner and deep respect for instructing "the simple people" in the principles of faith.

He was born on April 7, 1506, at the castle of Xavier, to a family of nobility; his mother was a heiress and his father was counselor to the king of Navarre. He showed an aptitude for learning at a young age and attended the College of St. Barbara in Paris. It was there he met and befriended Ignatius of Loyola, and soon he shared Loyola's vision of dedication to the service of God. He helped found the Society of Jesus. In 1537, Xavier was ordained to the priesthood, and three years later he was appointed by the king of Portugal to minister to people of the East Indies.

Over the next ten years, St. Francis Xavier established missions in regions of India, China, and Japan that had been considered too dangerous and foreign by the Catholic Church. Xavier relished the opportunity to travel; he quickly became fluent in the languages and ministered to the needs of the people, both rich and poor. He endured many physical hardships and was persecuted for his candid appraisals of the exploitation of natives by Portuguese settlers.

St. Francis died on an offshore Chinese island in December 1552. After his burial, the body of St. Francis Xavier was exhumed on three separate occasions and his remains examined by a myriad of physicians and clerics. These examinations remarked on the pristine condition of the body, and word quickly spread about the "miraculous condition of his body." Many countries lobbied the Society of Jesus for possession of the body. In 1614, after much deliberation, the Society of Jesus ordered Xavier's right hand—which he had often used in the ritual of baptism, for healing the sick, and effecting miracles—to be severed from his body and brought to Rome. The arm has never decayed and is declared a relic of this saint. The remains of his mummified body are enshrined in a church in Goa.

ST. FRANCIS XAVIER AT THE CASA

We recall a notable surgery that was taped by the Casa staff in November 2001, when St. Francis Xavier incorporated during a power outage. He worked by flashlight, performing many extraordinary surgeries. A woman from Heather's group complained of severe chronic tooth pain. Xavier pierced her right cheek with a metal probe, made a small incision in the gum, and applied a single suture. He then removed the pointed metal probe from her cheek. There was no entry or exit wound, not even a single drop of blood throughout the entire procedure. The Casa video shows her standing fully erect, calmly stating she experienced no pain. Before leaving, the Entity extended his right hand, and a Casa medium identified him as St. Francis Xavier.

On another occasion, St. Francis Xavier incorporated and proceeded to take crutches away from several people who approached him. As the crutches clattered to the floor, he lifted a wheelchair-bound person and invited him to walk out of the room. He then came down the line, personally addressing people with messages of healing. When he approached Heather, he extended his right arm with his palm facing her and asked, "Filha, who am I?" The words "Francis Xavier" blurted from her mouth. Later on, Xavier shared stories of miraculous healings he had performed with his right arm when he was in the physical.

On April 29, 2006, a visitor to the Casa announced she had gifts for the Entity. The first was a statue of Santa Rita from the monastery in Cascia. Next she unwrapped a beautiful painting of Francis Xavier, which she had brought from the chapel in Rome where his hand is on display. The Entity changed and Francis Xavier came through. He was very pleased with the painting, and Heather asked him if it was a good likeness. He smiled with great delight and said that indeed it was. He then asked if anyone knew the story of what happened to his arm in that lifetime. Xavier stood from his chair and pointed to his arm, indicating the exact location where it had been severed, just below the elbow. He then graciously thanked the woman and asked that she hang the painting on the wall behind his chair.

KING SOLOMON

King Solomon was born in the tenth century B.C., the tenth son of King David and Bathsheba. His forty-year reign over the Israelites is recorded in I Kings and II Chronicles. During this time, Solomon placed his efforts on expanding the borders of his kingdom. His greatest accomplishment was the completion of the Holy Temple, a monument erected to preserve the Ark of the Covenant on Mount Mariah. The Temple represented a sacred sanctuary, where the Jewish people could freely commune with God in accordance with religious rituals and pilgrimages. The Temple was therefore seen as a pinnacle of success based on religious, political, and commercial criteria.

Solomon is attributed with having written the books of Proverbs and Ecclesiastes. Many secular stories remark on Solomon's wisdom and fairness as a ruler. One of the most popular accounts describes two women who came to Solomon seeking his judgment over a dispute. These women argued over a small child; each woman stating she was the rightful mother. King Solomon decreed he would cut the child in half. Upon hearing this ruling, the true birth mother relinquished her rights to the child, begging Solomon not to harm the child. Upon hearing her words, Solomon presented the woman with the child.

This reference to Solomon as the "wisest of all men" is most likely inspired by a biblical passage in I Kings. Solomon, age twelve, is asked by God what he desires as a newly appointed king of Israel. Solomon requests the gift of an understanding heart, to which God replies,

> *Because you have not requested riches and honor but only that which would benefit all people, I will give you not only an understanding heart like none other before or after you...but also riches and honor like no other king in your days.*[3]

Perhaps it was this compassionate, understanding heart that healed over forty people on that remarkable day at the Spiritist Center of Christ the Redeemer, where Medium João first incorporated this Entity of Light in the late 1950s.

SAINT RITA OF CASCIA (1381–1457)

Often referred to as the "Saint of the Impossible," Saint Rita of Cascia is worshiped by those who bear exceptionally heavy burdens in their life, most notably women. This is because Saint Rita endured suffering in her roles as wife, mother, widow, and ultimately

3. I Kings 3:11–13.

religious worshiper—as evidenced by her austere practices as an Augustine nun.

Born in the small village of Roccaporrena, Italy, Rita Lotti was the only daughter of elderly, devout Catholic parents. Rita's one desire was to be of service to God. She often visited the convent of Augustinian nuns in Cascia and hoped to join their community. Her parents had other plans for her future. They arranged for her to marry a man they believed would provide her with a secure, happy, family life. Rita was bitterly disappointed but came to believe it was God's will that she marry. She entered into the union with a most reverent attitude, wholeheartedly accepting her new duties as wife and mother. Unfortunately, her husband proved to be ill-tempered and abusive. Prayer and patience filled her days as Rita endured a difficult life.

The death of her husband, a result of violent brawl, brought Rita more grief: her two young boys sought to avenge their father's murder. Rita patiently counseled her children, instructing them in prayer and forgiveness. When this failed, she prayed to God, asking for God to intercede on her behalf. Within a year, both sons died and Rita began to devote her life to charitable works. She returned to the convent in Cascia, pleading with the nuns to accept her. At first, the nuns refused her request. Perhaps they feared the scandal that surrounded her husband's death; perhaps they refused to overlook the rule that novices should be virgins. However, as time passed, Rita was able to convince the nuns to accept her into their order. Some say that Rita was able to reconcile the families involved in her husband's death; another story states that Rita would sit in front of the convent gates, engrossed in prayer. One morning, the nuns found Rita within the walls of the convent, unable to explain how she had gained entry through the locked gates. Regardless of which story one believes, Rita received the order of the habit in 1413.

Her meditations and prayers showed a singular devotion to the suffering that Jesus endured on the cross. One day as she prayed, a wound appeared on her forehead where the crown of thorns would have laid; it is said that this stigmata stayed with her for fifteen years. In the final days of her life, St. Rita fell ill and was confined to her bed. It is said that one winter Rita asked a visitor to bring her a rose from her garden. When the visitor entered the garden at Roccaporrena, she was astonished to find a single rose on an otherwise dead rosebush. To commemorate this miracle, roses are blessed each year in all the churches of the Augustinian Order and offered to the faithful.

St. Rita of Cascia died in 1457 and was canonized in 1900. This beloved spiritual being, known for her forgiving spirit, appeared to Medium João in Mato Grosso in his youth, inspiring him to engage in a lifelong service to God.

DR. BEZERRA DE MENEZES (1831–1900)

Dr. Bezerra de Menezes was born in the State of Ceara, Brazil, on August 28, 1831. He received his medical degree in 1856 and soon after engaged in a political career that lasted nearly thirty years. He was an outspoken member of Brazil's Liberal Party. He was a successful business entrepreneur and founded the railway company Macahe & Campos.

A member of the Spiritist movement, Dr. Menezes, along with his friends and colleagues Caibar Schutel and Eurípides Barsanulfo, spread the "Good News" that death does not exist but is a transition from the material into the spirit world. He was proclaimed president of the Brazilian Spiritists Federation in 1894. Dr. Menezes is lovingly known as "Brazil's Allan Kardec" and the "doctor for the poor."

Dr. Menezes was the author of several spiritual books and is renowned for his charitable works. He had no set fee for his medical services and never turned anyone away. He was quoted as saying, "Doctors who deny assistance to people in need for any reason, especially financial, are in the business of healing and are not worthy to use the title 'Doctor of Medicine.'" Dr. Menezes came from a wealthy family, but he died a pauper on April 12, 1900, having spent his fortune tending to the sick and the poor.

DR. AUGUSTO DE ALMEIDA (d. 1908)

It is not sufficient to believe, it is necessary above all
to be examples of goodness and tolerance.

—Dr. Augusto de Almeida

Dr. Augusto is one of the most frequently incorporated Entities at the Casa de Dom Inácio. He reports that he held different occupations in previous incarnations; he worked in the military, was a rubber taper, and became a physician. When Dr. Augusto incorporates, his strong personality and authoritarian manner are most readily noticed. He works in a serious and quick manner, does not like to be interrupted as he works, and expects order and respect. During his life as a doctor, he witnessed much suffering because anesthesia had not yet been invented. He has remarked that his patients would endure the pain of surgery by biting on bits of wood or pieces of thick cloth. As an enlightened spirit, he is dedicated to alleviating pain and suffering. Dr. Augusto is extremely kind, and he is deeply loved by everyone at the Casa.

In 2004, Dr. Augusto called Martin Mosqueira and Heather to his side, explaining that it had been ninety-six years since he had disincarnated (died). He said in that lifetime he had lived in a small community in Jacunda, in the State of Para, where he was working on a gold-mining project with a group of Europeans. "Then everything went wrong," he said. He seemed to be lost in the memory for a few minutes. "To this day there is a very small chapel there, but it is now almost submerged in water." On Easter in 2003, Dr. Augusto announced that he had been elevated to another level and he was now the "sheriff" of that particular spiritual realm.

DR. OSWALDO CRUZ (1872–1917)

Dr. Oswaldo Cruz was born in the State of São Paulo on August 5, 1872. He began his studies at the Faculty of Medicine of Rio de Janeiro at the age of fourteen, graduating five years later as a medical doctor. His thesis was on the subject of water as a transporter for the spread of microbes. Subsequently, he specialized in bacteriology at the Pasteur Institute in France.

He was the founder of the Federal Serotherapy Institute, now known as the *Oswaldo Cruz Institute*, which produced vaccines against the bubonic plague, yellow fever, and smallpox. The Brazilian government asked the Pasteur Institute in Paris to send a specialist to help with these epidemics. The answer from the Pasteur Institute was that Brazil *already* had the best man available: Dr. Oswaldo Cruz. He was instrumental in initiating sanitary campaigns throughout Brazil, which were successful in arresting epidemics in Rio de Janeiro and other cities, thereby saving thousands of lives.

Dr. Cruz was appointed director general of public health in 1903. Dr. Carlos Chagas, one of his students, discovered a parasite responsible for the condition known as *Chagas' disease*. This parasite bears Cruz's name, *Trypanosoma cruzi*.

In 1907, at the 14th International Congress on Hygiene and Demography in Berlin, Germany, Dr. Cruz was awarded a gold medal in recognition of his achievements. After his retirement as minister of health in 1909, he focused on the Oswaldo Cruz Research Institute in Manguinhos, Rio de Janeiro, where he organized scientific explorations into the interior of Brazil and brought back important information about the indigenous peoples. He also implemented sanitation programs in Belem in the State of Para and the Vale de Amazonas region of Brazil.

Suffering from renal disease, he retired from his medical career to the city of Petropolis in the State of Rio de Janeiro. He became honorary mayor of the city in 1916. He died on November 11, 1917, at the age of forty-five.

As an Entity at the Casa, Dr. Cruz is known to be direct and forthright in his interactions, while at the same time he is extremely kind and compassionate. He has the most beautiful eyes, which seem to pour out unconditional love toward everyone around him. He rarely announces himself by name, but he is recognized by his manner and interest in viral and difficult diseases. He will often request that wristwatches be removed because it disturbs his current.

Heather relates that one time Dr. Cruz asked a volunteer to let him hold a wristwatch the volunteer was wearing. He was proud of this fine imported timepiece, and he quickly gave it to Dr. Cruz. Later that day, the man noticed his watch had stopped. He took it to the jeweler to have the battery replaced. When the watch was opened, the man found the internal workings were warped and twisted. Months later, the Entity Dr. Cruz summoned him, asking if he was still carrying his watch. The man said yes, hoping the Entity would ask to hold it and perhaps repair it. Dr. Cruz smiled and asked the man if he would part with the watch. The man agreed. Dr. Cruz briefly held the watch in his hand and then gave it to another person. The wristwatch began to tick, fully restored.

On another occasion, the Entity Dr. Cruz was attending people in the south of Brazil. A man of little means was asked by the Entity to come to the Casa for further treatment. He replied he did not have the money to do so. The Entity Dr. Oswaldo Cruz took the watch from Medium João's wrist and gave it to the man, saying, "Sell this and you will have more than you need for the journey to the Casa."

DR. JOSÉ VALDIVINO

There is a photograph in the surgery room at the Casa where we can see the Entity Dr. José Valdivino so fully incorporated that João's physical body is almost completely overshadowed by the

Entity. Very little is known about Dr. Valdivino, who when asked, replies simply that he was a "protector of families."

Medium João believes Dr. Valdivino was a legal judge in one of his lifetimes. He is extremely gentle, compassionate, and loving, and he possesses energy that is especially powerful for healing paraplegics. With a touch of his hand and a command for them to walk or move an afflicted limb, many miraculous healings have occurred.

ANDRE LUIZ

Andre Luiz was a practicing medical doctor during the early twentieth century in Rio de Janeiro, Brazil. This discarnate spirit is known for his valuable contributions on the nature of the afterlife. His most memorable accounts were psychographed by the medium Francisco C. Xavier and translated into English. The first book is a personal account entitled *Nosso Lar: A Spiritual Home*, which provided the first detailed account of life in the spirit world and candidly shares reflections on his life, his after-death experiences, and his struggles in discarding his beliefs about the nature of death. His working relationship with Xavier continued during this time. Luiz shares many of his attitudes and insights in this work. In his second book, *And Life Goes On...*, Luiz shares his observations on the meaning of love and friendship and the various roles each plays in a person's spiritual growth.

SISTER SHEILA

Sister Sheila was a nurse during World War II. She was born in Germany and tirelessly helped the German victims during that time. She died in an air raid near the end of the war. When the Entity or spirit of Sister Sheila is in the Casa, the strong scent of roses is also present.

EURÍPIDES BARSANULFO (1880–1918)

Eurípides was born and lived his entire life in the small town of Sacramento in the State of Minas Gerais, Brazil. He was a politician, journalist, and educator. Eurípides soon developed a reputation as a compassionate and dedicated teacher. He co-founded a primary and secondary school in his hometown.

Eurípides was brought up to be a devoted Catholic, but he became fascinated with the writings and teachings of Allan Kardec. He ran a Spiritist Center for twelve years and then founded the renowned Allan Kardec College in 1907. His healing and mediumistic abilities were internationally known. Eurípides was a devoted follower of the teachings and principles of Jesus and dedicated his life to service. He worked tirelessly throughout the Spanish influenza epidemic helping thousands. Exhausted and weakened from the extended effort, he died on November 18, 1918, at the age of thirty-eight.

FRANCISCO CÂNDIDO XAVIER (1910–2002)

Francisco Cândido Xavier was born in the city of Pedro Leopoldo, in the State of Minas Gerais, Brazil, on April 2, 1910. Known affectionately as Chico Xavier throughout Brazil and Latin America, he is one of the most prolific twentieth-century writers in Brazil's Kardecist Spiritist movement. He is noted for his amazing paranormal abilities as a medium, most notably the technique referred to as *psychography*: channeling a spirit in order to write a book based on the knowledge imparted by the spirit. It is unclear whether or not Chico is one of the many incorporating spirits at the Casa. He was a mentor and beloved friend of Medium João.

Chico has channeled over four hundred books that cover a wide range of subjects. He is most noted for the works he produced in collaboration with two of his guides: Emmanuel, a highly advanced being who shares his vision of a new form of Christianity, and Andre Luiz, a physician and poet who commented on the nature of life after death. His books have sold over 25 million copies, and all profits are donated to charity. In addition to his work as a medium, Chico Xavier dedicated his life to Jesus, was an avid humanitarian, and devoted his psychic abilities to reassure others that life continues after death.

Chico Xavier predicted that when he disincarnated, Brazil would be engaged in "a day of celebration." Chico died on June 30, 2002, at the age of ninety-two. That very day, Brazil won the World Cup for the fifth time; indeed, the entire country was engaged in a day of celebration. The country still mourns the loss of their beloved Chico. During his two-day wake, it is estimated that approximately 2,500 people per hour paid tribute to him as they filed past his coffin. Among those in attendance were Brazilian as well as Islamic, Jewish, and Christian world leaders. Chico's books are rich and enlightening, and they are most helpful if you intend to visit the Casa. Chico Xavier's works are being translated and are available from *www.sgny.org.*

EMMANUEL

The enlightened being known as Emmanuel was Chico Xavier's spiritual guide and mentor. According to Chico, Emmanuel lived as Senator Publius Sentulus during Roman times. Another of his many incarnations was in Portugal, in 1517, as Manuel de Nobrega, an important leader in the Jesuit movement. Nobrega was sent to convert the indigenous people of Brazil and to create colleges and schools. He was a prominent figure in Brazilian history with regard to the founding of the city of São Paulo. Emmanuel is also reported by Chico to have had a life as a professor at the Sorbonne. Emmanuel does not often announce himself, but he is one of the Entities who incorporate through Medium João.

When Emmanuel first appeared to Chico to prepare him for his mission, he asked Chico if he was ready for the task. Chico's reply was affirmative. Emmanuel promised never to abandon him and gave Chico three rules to follow on his spiritual mission:

1. Discipline
2. Discipline
3. Discipline

SPIRITUALISM

Spiritualism and Spiritism both share the belief that communication with the deceased is possible. The spirits are contacted through mediums, who communicate directly with these spirits to bring through messages, guidance, support, and teachings. Spiritualism does not follow a particular doctrine. Spiritism is a collection of tenets and lessons taken directly from highly evolved spirits, such as Jesus. These teachings comprise the philosophy and practice of Spiritism, referred to as the *Spiritist Doctrine*.

ALLAN KARDEC (1804–1896)

> *To be born, to die, to be reborn yet again and constantly progress.*
>
> —Allan Kardec

Allan Kardec was born in Lyon, France, in 1804, as Hippolyte Léon Denizard Rivail. A well-educated man, he spent his early life steeped in the academic pursuits of science, medicine, and the classics. By the mid-1800s, Kardec's interest focused on the supernatural phenomenon of spirit communication: the alleged ability of spirits to physically make their presence known. Fascinated by this topic, Kardec compiled a list of questions and began working with renowned mediums and channelers in an attempt to scientifically record these phenomena. By 1857, his research findings were published in the French text, *Le Livre des Esprits*. This treatise was Kardec's first attempt to offer a precise explanation of the relationship between the spiritual and material worlds.

There are some who take a dualistic view of the world, maintaining that physical reality is the domain of science and all else falls to religion. Spiritism seeks to bridge this chasm by offering a unique perspective on the interconnectedness of both domains. Kardec believed that all authoritative institutions, science and organized religion, were incapable of objective studies of paranormal phenomena because both were too steeped in dogma. His intention was to understand the relationship *between* the physical and nonphysical worlds based solely on spiritual discernment. Starting from the premise that the soul is eternal, his research was aimed at clarifying the state of the soul throughout each incarnation. His research formed the basis of the Spiritist doctrine, which adheres to the belief that only direct communication with the spirit world provides objective answers to the question of how to live a moral and ethical life. The complete set of principles is expounded in a series of five books, offering us valuable insights on the purpose and meaning of our lives.[4]

In its most basic sense, the Spiritist doctrine deals with the existence of the soul and its state after death. It begins with the premise that an Entity, or spirit, is an intelligent force with a will of its own. Direct communication with these spirits is conducted with the singular purpose of advancing our individual and collective spiritual progress. As a *practice*, the doctrine offers a precise set of tools and guidelines we can use to either bear witness to these communications or enter into fruitful and safe communications with these spirits. The objective of those who engage in such communications (mediums) is to employ their mediumistic abilities in a direct and useful manner.

The *philosophical* underpinnings of the doctrine comprise the actual teachings of the spirits. Much like us, these spirits are involved in a journey to attain higher and purer realms of consciousness. And because of this, they freely offer us the lessons they have learned, lessons that are ultimately intended to clarify the relationship between God and ourselves. This relationship is usually referred to as the *void*, or *hiatus*, in the Spiritist doctrine. To quote Kardec,

It is the Spiritist Doctrine that fills this hiatus. It shows us that all things are linked together from one end of the chain to the other; that beings,

4. See Bibliography and Suggested Reading, page 200, where Kardec's books are listed.

existing on an infinite number of levels, fill the void between God and ourselves; and that these beings are spirits like ourselves, each at a different point on the path of progress.[5]

For those of us who journey to Abadiânia, this void is filled by the loving and compassionate Entities at the Casa de Dom Inácio de Loyola. Medium João, who is devoted to a life of spiritual service, is the vehicle through which healing is given and received—by all of us, regardless of how far we have progressed on our spiritual journey.

5. Allan Kardec, *The Spirits' Book*, 31.

MIRACULOUS HEALINGS

Healing requires: Patience, Perseverance, Persistence, and Faith.

—Dr. Augusto de Almeida

Throughout the course of twelve months, over one hundred testimonials were collected for this book. The stories came from people we personally knew or had seen at the Casa, or people the Entities told us we should speak with. We wish it were possible to include every one of them, but there simply is not enough space for them all. We are grateful to everyone who took the time to share his or her remarkable healing experiences. To share these with you now, exactly as they were conveyed to us, is both an honor and a privilege.

▲

A CALL TO HEALING
Phillip C. Bechtel, M.D.

I have been a neurosurgeon practicing in Fort Worth, Texas, for the last thirty years, and I also have an interest in alternative healing methods, seeking ways to combine them or look for the fundamental healing patterns in concert with standard medical practice.

I eventually began to feel a pull toward South America and, ultimately, heard about a man called *John of God*. My initial trip was in February 2002, when I traveled with tour leader Heather Cumming. Over the next two years, I went to Brazil a total of eleven times.

At the time of my initial visit, I watched John of God make incisions on people as well as scrape their eyes and place hemostats up their noses without significant pain and with very little or no bleeding and no sign of infection. This forced me to ask the question, "How could this be?" It was in the asking of this question that my mind opened to the possibility that there might be more to this than just some bizarre set of practices.

During my first week at the Casa, I was called in front of the Entity and asked what I smelled with my eyes closed. Initially, I thought it was some type of perfume, but I finally blurted out, "a peach rose." With this, the Entity indicated that he would teach me to do these surgeries. He instructed me to get a pen with either gold or silver in it and bring it to him. When I did this, he held it for a minute and then handed it back to me, telling me that he had put energy into it. He also told me I should use it in my work, but only for my most difficult cases.

I had no idea as to how to use the pen or the energy. I decided that with regard to the pen, I would use it when I felt apprehensive about a particular patient. I began to tell some of my patients about John of God and the pen he had given me. I asked them if they would like me to use the pen. No one ever refused. I would then simply sit with the patient in the holding area before surgery, holding the pen in one hand and then putting my hand and on the area where I was going to do their surgery. The energy always seemed to show up and go out of my hand and into the patient. After some time had passed, I would stop and we would resume the usual schedule of events with regard to surgery. I have never used this technique as an alternative to standard medical care in my practice. Rather, I have used it in a complementary fashion. I have had a number of experiences using the pen over time, perhaps totaling 800 sittings.

With each trip to Brazil, I would be told to sit in the current room, where I would receive energy. From time to time, I would be given an assignment to work with a specific person. The first of these was a quadriplegic woman from France with multiple sclerosis. I was told to put my hand on the back of her neck and sit by her for two hours. The Entity said that at some point, something would "come into me." He also stated that I might lose consciousness. Because of this, he would have another medium standing behind me in the event that I might fall. As you can suppose, this was somewhat disconcerting and a little frightening. However, I did meet with the woman and followed his instructions.

Something did come into me about an hour and fifteen minutes into the sitting. It was an energy that I had experienced before in another place involving a Native American healing ritual using a mask. From this, I understood that the healing energy of the Entities is transcultural. Before I left, following this assignment, John of God said, "Now that you know what the energy is, work with it."

In addition to my trips to Brazil, there have been innumerable occasions when I experienced the work back home in Texas, usually at night. For a long time, I had a series of dreams in which I talked with John of God. He would ask me questions and I would answer. I would then awaken and experience an hour or so of intense energy and then fall back asleep. On occasion, I would awaken with severe pain in one of my legs. This pain was so intense I could hardly bear it. I would ask myself, *I wonder if they are working on me?* At that very instant, the pain would go away. This happened three or four times. I believe my body was being physically changed to accommodate the conduction of the energy. Over time, I was able to tolerate more and more energy without undue side effects, other than a transient difficulty concentrating and some clumsiness, which lasted for fifteen to twenty minutes.

At the time of my last trip to Brazil, it seemed as if the Entities were done with me—at least in terms of visits to the Casa. They acted as if I did not exist, and they had no further instructions for me. Then the intuitive knowledge came to me that I was complete in terms of the spiritual work I had been doing in Brazil. It has been two years since I was last there. At one point, I asked John of God, "When should I return?" and he responded, "Whenever you think." Many of his responses to me have held double meanings, and in this case I realized that perhaps the underlying message was that I could always return to Brazil simply by thinking about it.

At the same time that I stopped going to Brazil, I stopped using the pen. With some apprehension, I put it away in a nice leather box and left it there, except from time to time, when I look at it and remember using it. I began the work using just my hands, along with the pen. I eventually came to the conclusion that the pen was like a pair of bicycle training wheels, which are very useful to get you going. At some point, the wheels are taken off and you discover that you can stay up on your own and that you are much more mobile. This has been the case with the energy and my hands. I have continued with my work, and the energy has continued to be there whenever I am in a situation when I need it. I am always aware of a low level of continuous energy, but when I summon it with a simple prayer, it always comes. There has been only one occasion when it did not appear. At that time, I was working with a woman who was dying and absolutely nothing came. I took this to mean there was to be no interference with the events that were transpiring; it did not represent a failure of the work I was doing.

I employ this work in a very simple way: I hold the patient's hand, make contact with my knees, and use water and a small candle. I say a prayer asking God to place my hands in his, so that when I reach out to touch the patient it is God's hands that are touching them. This prayer encapsulates the sum total of the healing function of John of God. When I say this prayer, the energy immediately comes. It runs a variable length of time, usually about twenty to thirty minutes, and then stops abruptly on its own without any interference from me.

I do not know what the energy is or how it works. Indeed, I have been informed in the current room that I am not supposed to know, and this is enough of an answer for me. I have noticed that the energy seems to set up a sympathetic vibration in the person whose hand I am holding. This makes me wonder whether I am triggering a force inside the patient that generates healing. I have come to the conclusion that my job is simply to get out of the way and serve as a conduit of this energy, or force. I firmly believe that the source from which the energy comes knows far more about what to do, where to go, and how to help the person I am working with than I do. Therefore, I do not attempt any direction or control of the energy, or its function within the patient.

Although most of my work has been directly in contact with another person, there have been many instances when I have worked with people at a distance in exactly the same way. They report experiences that rival or at times exceed the physical experience of direct work. I have done this type of work in places as distant as Brazil, Costa Rica, California, Washington, Canada, and New Mexico.

I work primarily with people who have cancer, but I am not able to claim any cures. There has been a substantial amount of pain relief, and I believe that survival of these patients may well be longer, certainly in the malignant brain tumor population, but ultimately they have all passed away. The incredible thing for me has been the connection I have experienced with my patients doing this work. It is one of the most deeply intimate and human things I have ever done.

I think it is important to put forth the view that this work has very little to do with the healer. John of God frequently says that he is only a simple man and that God does the healing. It is a natural tendency of people who are ill to project onto a healer some part of themselves that has a tremendous need. If anything, I can only be grateful for the experiences I have had in Brazil and for the connection it has given me with my own patients here in this country. John of God performs an enormous service to humanity at the Casa.

However, the ultimate point of the work he does is not about John of God but about the energy, the force, the spirits, the collective unconscious, or God behind all of it. This is what is really at work here, and in some way, it opens our consciousness to what is possible. I believe we are limited only by our imagination.

▲

DIVINE INTERVENTION
Marcelene Da Silva Oliveira

In September 2003, Marcelene Da Silva Oliveira felt she had no option but to have surgery to amputate her deformed arm. Two years before, her cancerous tumors had been removed, but the wounds would not heal. The open, gaping flesh was fetid and beginning to rot. Her arm lay against her waist, limp and immobilized. The previous surgery had removed her tendon, and now her arm did not respond.

In early October 2003, Sebastian asked Heather to translate Marcelene's story. The month before, he had photographed her arm. Sebastian could not believe his eyes when he saw the extensive healing that had taken place. The wounds were almost closed and healthy tissue was forming. Halfway through Marcelene's story, Sebastian held up the photograph and everyone gasped because the photo so vividly depicted the putrid flesh.

Marcelene tells her story:
When the doctors told me that the bulges on my arm were very bad tumors and that if the disease went to my brain I would die, I gave them permission for surgery. In removing the cancer they cut

150

out the nerve and tendon of my hand. It has been useless here at my side ever since the operation two years ago. I am unable to move it up or down. My wounds, as you can see from the picture, were gaping, foul-smelling, and almost an inch wide. I was in extreme pain and depression. The doctors told me the only solution was to amputate my arm to prevent further infection. The appointment for surgery was made for the following Monday morning.

On Friday, a friend who works at the Casa insisted that I see John of God before losing my arm. I live only two hours away, but I did not know about John of God and the generous spirits here. It is financially difficult for us to travel and to leave home, but my brother came immediately and brought me to the Casa.

Heather continues:

All the staff at the Casa was amazed at Marcelene's recuperation in just thirty days. This is such a powerful testimony of the potency of one visit to the Entity and the healing power of the herbs. It was a renewal of faith for us all, and we could sense the elevated energy and excitement all day.

Marcelene asked me to take her to the Entity; she was shy, but she very much wanted to honor and thank the Entity. Standing before the Entity, she showed him her arms and the miraculous result of the work from only taking the herbs. He smiled with the compassionate knowing that reaches into the darkest crevices of our hearts. "This afternoon operation, I will do your work. And you have a problem here." He reached past Marcelene and momen-tarily massaged her brother around the liver area, "Your liver. I will do your work today and then you should go to the earth doctor to finish your treatment." We walked toward the surgery room. Her brother was white. He had an appointment for a liver scan and gall bladder removal already scheduled at the hospital.

I waited for Marcelene at surgery time and then accompanied her and her brother to their car. Karen grabbed the video, and

Marcelene began to tell her story. Suddenly she realized that she was touching her mouth with her left hand, which had been paralyzed for two years! "My God! My arm and hand are moving!" she exclaimed in tears. Her movements were slow and stiff, but a week later, when she returned for surgery revision, she had complete and fluid movement of the whole area. Marcelene is amazed that her arm responds and moves without the tendon and with a severed nerve. She returns to the Casa once a month for healing. It is a day's work for her brother who is a taxi driver. Marcelene cannot work and would not be able to afford to visit the Casa regularly. Our commitment to her is to ensure she has funds for transportation in advance so she can make regular visits and continue her treatment. She is dedicated to the Casa and always brings her family and friends in need. Marcelene is courageous, kind, and has incredible faith. It gives us faith to hear these powerful testimonials.

"I return to give thanks and bring my uncle, cousin, and niece," says Marcelene. "My uncle had the same kind of tumors in his arm. Now they have all been removed by the Entities. It took but a few minutes; there was no bleeding, and they looked like mere scratches compared to the deep scars I suffered. His hernia is still bulging, but he has no pain. My niece had frequent epileptic fits, but she is now well after only one visit. My cousin had a stomach disorder, and he is feeling better. There are no thanks great enough for the Divine Love that is here. I will return as often as I can to sit in current and pray for all those who come here to be healed."

▲

NO MORE LEG BRACES—NO MORE CATHETERS
Ana Lucia

Ana Lucia was born in 1985 with spina bifida and dislocation of the hips. From birth, her legs were extended above her head and touching her ears. She was not able to bring them down or stretch them out like a normal child. It took the doctors a month and a half to straighten her legs out. She had undergone eight surgeries by the age of four.

Ana Lucia begins her story:
I don't know why some children are born with this disease, but I was lucky in that it did not disrupt my brain function, except for a nerve missing to my bladder that prevented normal urinary function. My family had heard about the House of St. Ignatius when I was nine years old. For the first year, I could not physically make the long journey to Abadiânia, so we had a friend bring my picture to the Entities. I received herbal remedies, which I took faithfully. This was how the Entities treated me without my physical presence.

When I was ten years old, the Entities asked me to come to the Casa. I came with my family. I had two large braces on my legs that reached my hips. I used walking sticks and wore diapers. When I came before the Entity, I did not ask to be cured, but I told him that I could not come back every forty days because I lived far away in the south of Brazil. The Entity said, "My daughter, you can come every ninety days, and if I do not cure you I will close down this House."

For the next two years, I traveled thirty-eight hours by bus to see the Entity every three months. He would write out a prescription for herbs and I would return home. He never said anything to me. I followed the protocol judiciously. After two years, I asked him when I would have regular function of my bladder. Dr. Augusto informed me that when it was safe to remove the urinary bag and catheter he would tell me and I would be ready. Two days later, I left on the bus. I had a bladder infection, and once I removed the catheter to change it, I was unable to place it back inside because of the infection. I did not urinate, even in my diapers, for twenty-seven hours. When I got home, I suddenly felt a pressure to go to the bathroom, and I urinated normally for the first time without the catheter. The doctors said I could not live permanently without the catheter because there was a possibility of a backwash, which would be gravely detrimental to my kidneys. I called Sebastian at the Casa about my predicament. He went before Dr. Augusto, who told him that he would help me. I made the decision to not use the catheter again because I felt spiritually and physically prepared. I was fully cognizant that I carried the responsibility of my decision.

Four months later, in 1999, I returned to the Casa during my summer break from school for three months. Dr. Augusto told me to go on the little stage and give my testimony. He then called a doctor out of the current room to witness as Dr. Augusto took one of my crutches from me and threw it to the ground with a flourish. Dr. Augusto then told me to walk. I took a few steps but fell because I was used to having two crutches. Dr. Augusto told me to get up. He said I could do it, and no one was to help me because I was being imbued with healing energy. From that moment, I started walking with only one crutch and my two large braces.

In January 2002, I had a complete medical checkup with exceptional results. Finally, the large cumbersome braces were removed and I was given two small leg braces. Elated, I came to the Casa and handed over my large braces to the Entity on a Friday. The following Wednesday, I removed both small braces myself, realizing I no longer needed them. I donated them to the Casa. My bladder is completely healed: no diapers, no catheter. I still walk with small crutches but have free movement of my legs. Look, now I can even ride a bike. (Ana Lucia hopped on her bike and cycled off toward her hotel, waiving and giggling delightedly.)

At the time of this interview, in 2003, Ana Lucia was nineteen years old and a freshman in college. Now her focus is to walk freely without crutches.

▲

PROTECTION FROM THE FATHER
Tião Passarinho

At the end of an afternoon session in February 2005, Sebastian was eager to introduce Heather to his *xara* (one whose name is the same). He wanted her to listen to the story of Sebastião Pereira Dos Santos, fondly known as *Tião Passarinho* (also known as Sebastião). "Show her your scars from the bullet wounds first," he urged. "Then tell her your story." Tião lifted his shirt and the scars of four bullet wounds were clearly visible, one just above the heart, one in the area of the spleen, another by the right rib cage, and the fourth in the stomach area.

Tião Passarinho begins:

On October 14, 1994, I was bringing my son home from school in the early afternoon. I shall never forget that day. I was parking my taxi when another car drew up in front of me and the driver got out and began shouting at me. My son was sitting in the passenger seat beside me. I did not get out of the car because I feared for our lives. I knew this man; we had a falling-out over business. I noticed another man with a bright yellow shirt and brown pants standing by the car. He was on the passenger side. I thought he must be accompanying the enraged man. The driver of the car was now only about one meter from me. He had a gun in his hand and fired five shots. Four of the shots entered my body—the scars you see here are from the bullet wounds. One bullet was lodged in the car. I was rushed to a hospital, where I remained for seventeen days. I am lucky to be alive. I came to the Casa as soon as I was released.

Sebastian shares:

Now listen to this. I was on the stage with the Entity as he performed surgeries, and the Entity turned to me and said, "Go and get the filho, the one who is your friend and xara. He has just arrived." As I crossed the Prayer Hall, I knew intuitively whom the Entity meant, but I had no idea that Tião was at the Casa. I knew nothing of the incident or his hospitalization. I met him standing outside of the hall and brought him up to the Entity. The Entity Dr. Oswaldo Cruz put his hand on Tião's shoulder and said, "Filho, do you remember the day you were shot? There was a man standing by the car wearing a yellow shirt and brown trousers. That was me, Dr. Oswaldo Cruz."

Tião continues:

I am alive because Dr. Oswaldo Cruz kept those bullets from lodging deeper into my body. Imagine five shots from the distance of one meter. The Entity kept me safe. I owe my life to him. Of this I am convinced.

I first came to the Casa in 1980 because my father was suffering from intense headaches. The pain was so severe and continuous that he had been interned in the Santa Casa de Misericordia Hospital under observation. The doctors ran tests for twenty-three days, but they could not find the cause of his migraines. I had heard about John of God, and so I went to the hospital and asked the doctors for permission to take my father out for one day. I was granted my request as long as I returned him to the hospital that same night. They wanted to continue the battery of tests.

I brought my father immediately to the Casa and took him before the Entity, who put his hand on my father's head and told him to come back in the afternoon for surgery. My father ran outside to a quiet area in the garden and began to sob after receiving this blessing. He told me he felt immense energy when the Entity placed his hand on his head and his headache immediately disappeared. He stayed for surgery, and that evening I took him back to the hospital. I told the doctors what had happened and that my father no longer had headaches. The doctor ordered a scan and found sutures clearly visible down the side of his left temple, even though there was no sign of external entrance. My father has never had another headache since this surgery so many years ago.

Whenever I buy a new taxi, before ever taking a person for a ride, I bring the keys to the Entity. He puts them in his hand and blesses me for safety. Being a taxi driver is a dangerous career, especially at night. I have been held up three times, but I am always safe and never hurt. This is a House of God, and I will always come here.

▲

CURED OF HEPATITIS B WITH ONE VISIT
Susan Schinstine

I applied to get health insurance in July 2002. In August, I received a letter from the insurance company denying me insurance. They encouraged me to go to my doctor because my blood test indicated my liver functions were elevated. My doctor did a battery of tests, and I tested positive for hepatitis B. He sent me to an endocrinologist to see what could be done. In the meantime, I was devastated and depression set in. I was sick, really sick, and what made it worse was I had no idea how I got this illness. I thought perhaps I had contracted it during a vacation in Egypt.

I was getting acupuncture treatments at the time, but I had to tell my friend she could no longer treat me. She told me about a workshop she was giving on healing and asked me to attend. For some reason, it was very important that I be there. During the workshop, she began talking about John of God. Then I understood why attending her workshop had been so vital. I needed to find out about him.

I knew I had to go to Brazil to see this healer. My friend put me in contact with Heather Cumming, a sister of the Casa and trip leader. In February 2003, I went to Brazil to see John of God with a group of others. I knew he would help me. We arrived on a Monday and Heather met us at the airport and took us to

Abadiânia. She showed us around and told us what to expect and what we needed to do. We went to the Casa on Wednesday of the first week. When it was my turn, we went in front of the Entity and explained my diagnosis. I asked the Entity to help me with my healing. He had a soft smile and warm eyes. He said he would help me and that I needed to come back the next morning for surgery.

The next day, I sat in the surgery room with my right hand on my heart and the left in my lap so the Entities would know that I was accepting any help they felt I needed. In prayer, I asked them to help me. I felt a light movement going on inside of my body, almost like a tickle through my torso. Then it moved up the side of my neck into my ear. I remember thinking to myself: *Great. They're going to fix my ear.* I hadn't told them about the earaches I have when I lay on my left side.

After the surgery, I went back to my room and lay down to sleep on my left side. I had absolutely no pain whatsoever in my ear. I spent the remainder of my two weeks in Brazil sitting in current, giving and receiving energy. I knew in my heart that I had been healed.

In June, I went to my family doctor, who was upset that I hadn't been back to the specialist. I told my doctor I didn't care for the specialist so he sent me to a different one. It took six months to get in to see the new doctor. It was now January 2004. I told the new doctor I didn't believe I was sick, but he retested me for all of the hepatitis viruses. He asked me what I had done. I told him I had gone to a spiritual healer, John of God, and that he had healed me. Not totally convinced, he ran a very expensive test that could pick up even the smallest traces of virus in the bloodstream. This test also came back negative. The doctor said I didn't even have the residue left in my bloodstream that is always there after treatment. He said to come back in three months to be rechecked, and if I had any pain in my liver I should come back sooner. Three months later, the recheck was also negative.

My husband and I returned to Brazil in May 2004. I again went before the Entity to thank him for curing me. The Entity said I no longer needed to worry. I had been cured of hepatitis and didn't need to return unless I wanted to. Needless to say, I have gone back every year and will continue for as long as I am able. I feel at home at the Casa and miss the connection when I'm not there. I now go to the Casa to give energy to others, knowing there is always more I can achieve in myself. I pray that I can help others by holding current for them, as was done for me.

▲

WE ARE ALL INVITED TO THIS PARTY
Roger Kitzis

Roger was an orthodontist working in his father's business on Long Island. A fun-loving guy with little to worry about, he enjoyed life to the fullest. But then he began to lose the vision in one of his eyes. The last thing he thought about was multiple sclerosis. He had rarely been sick his entire life. Why would that change now? The diagnosis left him stunned but determined not to be ravaged by the disease. He began to search for a holistic approach to his healing.

Roger relates his story:
When I came to John of God in September 2001, I was sure I would be healed immediately.

It didn't happen. Not only that, others would go in front of the Entity and he would talk with them and tell them to "sit in current" or go to the waterfall. He basically just waved me through with no recognition. So, I sat in the current room for three days. I was baffled and totally confused. My mentality was *I am a New Yorker. I know I am with "the man."* It was like going to an amusement park, and I took the ride. I thought, *So give me the healing already.* No wonder the Entity didn't look at me.

The second time I went to the Casa, I felt ignored until the last day. I couldn't visualize anything. I repeated the same request over and over when I was in the current. I wanted a healing so I could go back to my previous lifestyle, which included a lot of partying. I was pretty unconscious. Then I experienced a powerful waking dream. Heather told me it meant I was at a turning point. We went in front of the Entity, and I thanked him for the dream. For the first time, I was overwhelmed with gratitude. The Entity, who I now called *Father*, smiled and said, "This is what I was waiting for; now go to work." I continued to sit in his current room and meditate.

On my third visit, I requested visible surgery. My scientific mind wanted proof. Maybe the physical surgery would bring instant healing. I received "the nose job." It was a little uncomfortable. No magic. Before I left, Heather asked the Entity, "This is his third trip to the Casa, Father. How many times does he need to come back?"

The Entity replied, "If he comes back one more time he will be healed." So, of course, by the time I landed in New York, I had already booked my fourth trip and returned immediately. I was excited and fell back into wanting to get better so I could be my old self again. Life was one big joke, and I wanted the excitement. Although my body was slowly shutting down, I was still struggling to hold on to things that were essentially not possible or important anymore.

During my next trip, I realized that healing *does* come in many forms. After three years, I had come to the realization that I wanted happiness and peace more than a physical cure. I asked the Entity for happiness rather than physical healing. By the time I landed back in New York, I had found a sense of inner peace I had never felt before. Happiness is when you can be grateful for anything.

My journey still includes a physical resolution to my health problems: treatment with vitamins, drugs, and holistic medicine, but the end result will be from *within*. John of God taught me to understand and appreciate that there is Source Energy and to immerse myself in it. We are all invited to this party. There are no exclusions or judgments. I am enough just as I am. I hope to regenerate myself so I can be of service to others.

▲

THE LAST PLACE I EVER WANTED TO GO WAS BRAZIL
Andy Rayson

I am forty-six years old and work in the oil business. Up until three years ago, I was the president of a 3,000-person division of a multinational company. I live in the Netherlands and have a wife, Regina, two small children, Rosie, age four, and Joe, age two, and our dog, Billy.

During Christmas 2002, I was diagnosed with Parkinson's disease after living with a tremor in my right hand for about a year. It got steadily worse over the next couple of years. Early in 2005, Reggie found some information on the Internet about John of God and told me about the miracles that were happening at his healing center. For some reason, this really got me angry because I didn't want to rely on "miracles" for hope. I told her I didn't want to talk about it again, but for some reason this normal conversation had left me quite disturbed. I put it out of my mind and decided the last place I would ever go was Brazil.

About a week later, my boss called me and asked me to consult on an acquisition he was looking at in Brazil. He needed me to be there within a couple of weeks. I had never been to Brazil before, and this was not part of my normal duties. I immediately thought about visiting John of God. Reggie was keen for me to go, and she contacted Heather Cumming, who had just received a cancellation for her next trip two weeks later. This coincided with my plans to the day.

I was an agnostic and also an engineer, so I always needed an explanation for everything. I was pretty skeptical about someone who performed miracles. But I went with an open mind. I decided not to read anything about John of God beforehand. I was late joining the group in Abadiânia, but Heather immediately took over and "mothered" me through the whole process. I was struck by the warmth and love generated by this group of very normal people, even before we got to the Casa.

The next morning, Heather took me to see John of God. She told me to sit on the stage near the front. Within minutes, the Entity appeared on the stage with a young guy who seemed to be in a trance. He then proceeded to shove the Kelly clamp up the guy's nose. The man seemed oblivious to what was going on and continued to smile. I was horrified. When I went up to John of God myself ten minutes later and he told me I was going to have an operation, I can tell you, I was pretty spooked and was ready to take the next plane home. Heather explained to me that the real work is done spiritually. The physical operations are for people who need physical proof that something is happening. She assured me that John of God would not perform a physical operation on me without my consent.

When I looked into his piercing blue eyes and he smiled at me, I knew everything was going to be OK. He invited me to sit in his current room. Heather whispered to me to keep my eyes closed and ask for the healing that I needed. After what seemed like five minutes but in reality was about three hours, I was told to open my eyes. I was in a complete daze, but I was filled with more emotional warmth than I had ever experienced. I broke down and cried like I had not done since childhood.

That afternoon, I received a spiritual operation. By this time, I was completely comfortable with participating. My heart and mind were open. The operation had no immediate physical or emotional impact. I returned to my room and slept for about thirty hours, only waking to eat the blessed soup that Heather brought to me. I'm sure my transformation began during this long sleep. I experienced many dreams connected with my healing.

Three days later, I went on a two-hour bus ride with Heather and the group to see the sacred sites of Brasília. As I sat quietly alone on the bus, I realized that my hand had stopped shaking for the first time in many years. I was very excited but didn't want to say anything in case the magic might break. The shaking started to come back two hours later, but it was much less than before.

I experienced wonderful events during the following week, including visits to the rejuvenating waterfall, the meditation journeys Heather took us on, and the amazing bonds of friendship within the group. I released many emotions during the crystal baths and discovered spirituality with the help of the many wonderful people at the Casa. I had made tremendous physical improvements by the end of my first visit, but even more important was my spiritual awakening. This continues to bring me higher levels of peace and happiness. I am convinced all of this is leading me toward a complete recovery.

My other symptoms included loss of smell, rigidity, severe muscle pain, loss of balance, and poker face. I had all the tests and three separate opinions, including one from the leading professor in Holland. They all confirmed I had Parkinson's. I refused to take medication because I was concerned about long-term effects and effectiveness. I explored many alternative approaches and relied heavily on craniosacral massages, biofeedback treatments, and acupuncture. I have not returned to these treatments for six months now. I practice yoga and meditate daily for about twenty minutes.

Recently, I visited my neurologist, a very open-minded lady. She is amazed that I have shown consistent improvement over the last six months. She told me that my condition has recovered 80 percent and appears to have stabilized. She advised me that my every-three-month visits are no longer required and to call when and if I need her.

I don't have contact with many people who have Parkinson's, but I'm convinced that people with this disease have a strong need to be in control of their life. I'm sure part of my recovery is being able to open up a little and relinquish some control over my life. This I got from Abadiânia. I will continue to return to the Casa every year.

▲

EYESIGHT RECOVERY
Bob Dinga

In 1986, I was diagnosed with a rare disease in the retina of the eye called *serpiginous choroiditis*. There were no drugs to combat this disease, and laser surgery was the only way to stop its progression. Following five laser surgeries over a thirteen-year period, I was designated as legally blind and told that it would be beneficial to start learning Braille. There was nothing more that could be done.

In November of 1998, my beloved partner, Diana Rose, read a book to me written by Robert Pellegrino-Estrich entitled *The Miracle Man*. When she was finished reading the book, I decided I must go to Brazil to receive my miracle from John of God. At this point, I could still read large print and could drive around the immediate community as long as I knew the way.

Believing that an instantaneous miracle would restore my eyesight, I hired a translator who spoke Portuguese and proceeded to the Casa de Dom Inácio in Abadiânia, Brazil, for a one-and-a-half-day stay. I sat in the current room twice the first day and received a spiritual operation in the surgery room on the second morning. While I was sitting in the surgery room, I felt someone blowing in my ear. I remember thinking they should be working on my eyes, not my ear. Since I did not understand the severity of my surgery and didn't feel anything, my translator and I proceeded to tour the countryside. We even spent many hours shopping for crystals in the city of Cristalina. This was exactly the opposite of what we had been told to do following surgery.

By the end of the day, I was exhausted and began to realize that the Entity had really performed a major operation on me. But it was too late. I had ignored the warnings, and my eyesight began to get worse. When I arrived home, my ability to read had diminished to almost zero without strong magnification and my ability to drive was gone. When asked if I would ever go back to Abadiânia, I answered "No; not unless I receive a clear message from God."

Approximately three weeks after my return, John of God came to me in a dream. When I asked him if I should return to the Casa, he said "Yes, two more times." Without the ability to read the monitors in the airports or the ability to speak Portuguese, I returned on my own in May 1999 for three days and again in August for three weeks. After the May trip, my eyesight returned to the level it had been before going in January. My eyesight dramatically improved after August.

I noticed that each time I returned from Brazil my eyesight would improve significantly but start to degrade again after a couple of months. In December 1999, I visited the Casa for three weeks and had my most profound experiences, insights, and improvement in eyesight. I returned home and resigned from my job. My eyesight has improved ever since. I can read for short periods of time and drive wherever I want to go, even in minimal lighting conditions. I lead a normal life again and work from my home office using my computer to communicate with people around the world who want to know more about the Casa de Dom Inácio and John of God. (Bob and Diana Dinga live in California and are official Casa tour guides.)

▲

TOUCHED BY A BUTTERFLY
Ricardo Bezada

Ricardo began to have pain in his shoulder in 1987. The pain increased, and he was finally diagnosed with a cancerous tumor. From 1989 to 1992, Ricardo had seven surgeries at Valhalla Hospital in

New York State. Even with their best efforts, the surgeons were unable to remove the entire tumor because it was enmeshed with the nerves of his shoulder and arm. By 1992, Ricardo was in agonizing pain and had lost all movement of his right arm.

Ricardo tells his story:
I had no more options. The doctors wanted to amputate my right arm so they could contain the spread of the tumor. I decided to visit my family in Peru before making such a weighty decision. They told me about a healer from Brazil whom the president of Peru had invited to our country to help contain a cholera epidemic. They said that the healer, John of God, had seen 15,000 people and the epidemic had been contained. I had already sought help from many healers and shamans in Peru and was not convinced John of God could heal me, but I didn't want to lose my arm and not be able to work.

In desperation, I bought a plane ticket to Brazil. I arrived at the Casa de Dom Inácio for the morning session and was greeted by Sebastian, a jolly fellow who saw that I was crying from pain. I had not slept properly in five years and was exhausted. Sebastian brought me in front of the Entity, who told me I was to have invisible surgery that afternoon.

Later that day, I was told to sit with many others in the surgery room. The Entity came in and said a prayer. During the surgery, I felt a slight fluttering of energy like being touched by a butterfly. I was free of pain when I left the surgery room, only minutes later. Almost in a daze, I walked up to Sebastian and said, "Where is my pain?" I was told to rest. I went back to my hotel and slept for three days. For years, I had been unable to straighten out my body and had a marked slumping on my right side, but I slept totally stretched out after this surgery.

I flew back to New York and was met by my wife. She was excited when she saw me because I was standing upright, something

I had not noticed myself. My body had stretched out normally because the pain was gone. The tumor was still there, and although I was exhilarated by the continuous lack of pain, I returned within one week to Abadiânia to continue the work.

I immediately went to the hall to see Medium João. When the Entity came out on the stage, he came to me and took my hand into his. When he unbuttoned my shirt, I felt a surge of energy at the site of the large tumor. When he finished removing my shirt completely, I looked at my shoulder and could see that the tumor was gone. The Entity told me to go to the notary's office in the little village and have my healing officially recorded.

I go to the Casa once a year to give thanks and receive healing energy. I have deep scars from my numerous surgeries but no mass. I continue to be healed and work in my construction company in New York.

▲

SHARING THE GIFT
Sirlei Lerner

Sirlei left Porto Alegre, in the State of Rio Grande do Sul in the south of Brazil, to come to the Casa for the first time in January 1994. She had been battling carcinoma in her right breast for three years. The doctors believed that removing a quarter of her breast (followed by radiation and chemotherapy) was the best course of action. Sirlei wanted no part of such an intrusive therapy.

Sirlei tells her story:
I did not believe in conventional medicine but rather a holistic approach. I began eating raw foods, studying macrobiotics, and using naturopathic medicines. After three years, I had developed seven small tumors in my breast. I would not give up my holistic approach, but I was becoming scared. A friend told me that she was

going to take me to the Casa de Dom Inácio de Loyola for treatment. I was not sure whether my Catholic faith would allow me to see a Spiritist healer, but my friend bought our bus tickets. By that time, I had become exceedingly desperate. After all, what was my other choice? I could not contemplate that. We made the thirty-hour bus trip to Abadiânia.

On Wednesday morning, I went to the Casa and walked before John of God. St. Ignatius was the Entity who incorporated that day. He smiled at me and told me I was a medium of the Casa. He said I would not die of cancer and not to be afraid. He would cure me, but it would take returning many times. He said that my alternative methods had saved my life. If I had allowed my breast to be cut, it would have spread the cancer in a ferocious way and the Entities would not have been able to heal me. My illness was from a completely spiritual cause, and conventional surgery would not have helped.

So, my treatment began. The first time the Entity (Dr. José Valdivino) worked on me, I was placed on the *maca* bed. I was told that when the spirit sends a person to the *maca* it is for deep energetic healing. Dr. Valdivino gathered many mediums around, including the other Spirits of Light that work at the Casa on the invisible realm, and showed them the cancer, saying that it was called *aranha*, meaning spider. "It is a very aggressive and angry spider," he said. Then, starting at my feet, he went up my body, explaining why I had cancer. Blood came out of my breast when he squeezed the large tumor.

Every forty days, I traveled by bus to come in front of the Entity; the long ride became routine. One time, the Entity (Dr. Valdivino) took a syringe and put it into the tumors and extracted a bloody liquid. Blood also came out of my nipple. The spirit said they were taking all of the cancer in my body and bringing it to one place, which is why the tumor continued to grow. A third time, Dr. Valdivino did spiritual surgery.

In 1996, the Entity (St. Ignatius) realized I was becoming anxious and told me to go and have a medical exam after twenty-one days. I went to the best oncologist in the south of Brazil. He was astounded because the tumor was so large it would not fit on the monitor screen, yet the rest of my body was totally healthy. My liver, kidneys, brain, and all of my other organs showed no sign of cancer. The doctor was shocked that after five years of *untreated* cancer it had not metastasized throughout my body. He said I was a miracle of nature because there was no explanation. Four years went by in this way.

In 1999, I moved to the city of Anápolis to be closer to the Casa. One day, when I went for my healing, the Entity was King Solomon, who had not incorporated into Medium João for eighteen years. He told me that I had been very patient—although I felt impatient and somewhat nervous. He said, "Daughter, if you had not been coming to the House so diligently, you would not be with us still." It had been eight years since my diagnosis, and the tumor was still growing. The Entity then told me to have conventional surgery. He said the spirits had done their work, and all the cancer had been brought to one spot and encapsulated. It was like a dried orange and could now be removed by a medical doctor.

My medical doctor said he could perform a mastectomy for me in August of that year, but he wanted me also to have chemotherapy and radiation. I refused and asked him if he would perform the surgery anyway. My doctor said normally he would not, but this was such an extraordinary case that he would do what I asked. He performed the mastectomy on my right breast where all the cancer was contained.

In 2000, I had another examination, and no cancer was found in my body. I have not bothered to keep checking because I know without a doubt that the Entities have completely healed me of my spiritual disease. Once a week, I go to the current room in the House and meditate to help in the healing of others.

I began to feel a great desire to paint, although I had never painted before. I took a half-year course in 1999. Paintings began to manifest through my brush depicting Mother Mary, St. Ignatius, and many of the other Casa spirits. I took another course in acrylics in 2002. The teacher said I needed to paint ten hours a day and become an artist, or I would develop breast cancer. I told him that I already had breast cancer, so the only thing left was to become an artist. I now paint ten hours a day. I believe a message was spoken through him because he did not know me. The Entities have asked me to paint them. They said I am a "painting medium" and this is my gift to share with the world. My entire life has been transformed, and I am so very happy.

Heather continues:

I asked Sirlei to paint Dr. Augusto, including this statement he frequently makes: "My phalange is not comprised of ten, nor of a hundred, but of thousands. I am the one that goes to the very depths of the Abyss to rescue one soul." She created a beautiful painting and brought it to me. I took the painting to the Entity (Dr. Augusto) to be signed. He remarked that it was indeed an excellent likeness, but he said, "My eyes were green, not honey-colored. Also, my hairline was not so receded and my hair fell longer over my ears. My moustache was a little less manicured. But it is very good."

Sirlei made the small changes he requested, and we took the painting to the Entity again. This time, Dr. Augusto smiled, signed the painting, and pronounced it perfect. He instructed that all future paintings of him should contain his common phrase. Sirlei kept her word, and all subsequent paintings have carried his decree. I have quite a collection of her channeled paintings. I always invited her to bring her paintings to the hotel when my groups arrived. They were sold immediately and more orders were taken. Many of her paintings were also sold at the pousadas in the village. Sirlei was the sole supporter of her children, and she was grateful that the Entities gave her this painting gift.

In October 2005, the Entities told Sirlei she must not drive the following week on Tuesday, Wednesday, or Thursday. For whatever reason, Sirlei ignored the warning of the Entities and drove her son to work. On her way home she miscalculated the distance as she turned onto a main road and her car hit a bus. She died instantly. Everyone at the Casa was devastated by the news. On the day of her passing, Martin, one of the mediums and a translator for John of God, asked the Entities about Sirlei. He wanted to know why she had died and whether she was now with them. They told him the accident was her soul's choice. They said she was in a spiritual hospital and they were taking care of her. He asked if she would be joining the phalange, and the Entity replied that she would after her recuperation period. A week or two before her death, Sirlei told us how wonderful it felt that over five hundred of her paintings were now in many countries around the world.

▲

WALKING THE PATH TO GOD'S PERFECT LIGHT
Kathy Clifford

I was forty-eight years old when I was diagnosed with breast cancer that had metastasized to my ribs and spine. I have undergone two rounds of radiation, five types of chemotherapy, and multiple surgeries that added five feet of scars to my abdomen. Cancer consumed three of my lumbar vertebrae, which made spine reconstruction necessary and required a year of recovery. During the hospital stay for this surgery, I experienced a clear and detailed wake-up call from God that completely changed my life. I have been transformed from a secular person to a spiritually centered one. From the time of my hospital stay, I have felt that spiritual healing would play a critical role in my recovery. However, I feel it is paramount to accept healing from whatever source it is offered. This may include conventional treatments, following a special diet, taking supplements, and having a daily spiritual practice.

At this point, I have received four invisible surgeries from the Entities. Each has had powerful physical and emotional effects. Within hours after the first surgery, a large bruise formed over my spine. We applied blessed water, which felt like liquid light sinking into my body. The bruise faded overnight to a lighter brown. I continue to apply holy water when I am in pain, and it helps a great deal. Other surgeries were followed by pain in my ribs, hips, and spine. A great emotional or spiritual release or insight follows the surgeries.

As is fairly typical, my healing began with emotional healing. As I lay in bed, I experienced a review of the events that had hurt me deeply during my life, presented in chronological order. For the first time, I was able to see them from a different perspective: without judgment. I was able to understand that those I felt hurt by were imperfect humans just like me, and they made mistakes just like I do. I understood that they did the best they could at the time. Being able to forgive these people lifted an enormous weight off my shoulders and brought me a great deal of peace. I was also able to seek forgiveness from others for my own past actions, which freed me from the guilt I had punished myself with over the years.

Healing energy from the Casa Entities has spread throughout my family, benefiting us all. My sister was in a terrible car accident several years ago; she was hit by a drunk driver. Crushed from the waist down, she has limited mobility and lives with great pain. She has received two invisible surgeries in her home in the United States during Mom's and my visits to Casa Dom Inácio. On the first occasion, she was awakened by an Entity lifting her foot up and manipulating her ankle. Her pain was diminished from that point on. The second surgery was a surrogate, where our mother at the Casa acted as a conduit for my sister at home. The next morning, my sister awoke to find a black and blue ankle and further help with her pain. My sister had no background or experience in spiritual healing.

I now understand the purpose of my life is to walk the path toward God's perfect light. The path is long and filled with what I used to consider insurmountable obstacles. I now think of them as stones. When I encounter one, instead of feeling punished or victimized, I see a new lesson to learn. I celebrate the lesson because it means I have progressed along the path and am prepared for greater learning. I study each stone with compassion and love, and once I gain better understanding the stone shrinks down into a small pebble I can hold in my hand. Its emotional power over me has disappeared. I examine the pebble from all sides, gaining a more thorough understanding. Then I am able to accept, change, forgive, and release the issue the stone represents. Once the stone shrinks to a tiny pebble, I place it in my pocket and carry it as a reminder of the lesson I have learned. Once my path is cleared, I continue moving forward toward the light. It is my life's work to transform stones into small pebbles and clear the pathway to God.

Now that I have a better understanding of Spiritism, I am able to see that cancer can be a gift. I used to be arrogant. The disease grabbed my attention. It has kept me focused on learning and improving myself as well as on sharing the insights I have acquired with others. The moment I was able to change how I viewed the disease was a huge breakthrough. Once I was able to see my life as a day at school and understand and accept that my spirit is infinitely long-lived, the magnitude of what was happening to me shifted. Even if my body dies, I will not die. I'll get another body and go back to school to continue learning. My purpose is to love, evolve, and be of service as much as I can in this lifetime, as I will also in the next. But my body will not die anytime soon. Three months after my first visit to Abadiânia, the cancer went into remission and has remained there ever since.

▲

AMAZING GRACE
Margaret Newton

Last night, as I hugged my pillow, I was transported back to Brazil through a memory. It was Sunday, and Arturo was at the front of the room, having suffered a stroke two days previously and surviving. "Thanks to the Entities I am alive," he said. Everyone laughed. His direct, matter-of-fact manner was appealing, and he created a message that touched each person.

I remembered voices ringing out in the Casa as we chose songs from a book. I had not been able to sing for years after my mother died, even though I went to the Kingdom Hall with my uncle, and the congregation sang at the beginning and the end of the service. Attending the Kingdom Hall became a living memorial to her memory. I was visiting what once was, and now was not. Overwhelming sadness filled me. I was always left with a hollow sensation. A void of emptiness cradled me as I stood there no longer hearing her strong voice over my shoulder, as I had all of my life. I used to tease her, saying she led the whole group with the power in her voice and that there would be no song without her. Later, I would realize these words were true.

When I sang "Amazing Grace" at the Casa, I heard again my mother's voice and felt the love I had known as a child when she sang so loud and clear. Tears rolled down my cheeks, bathing my soul. I did not utter a sound. I could not move. I realized how much joy there is in song, and there in the Casa I let joy take the place of grief. I sensed white rose petals all around me, as though they were a metaphor for light pouring into my body. The voices of small children could be heard singing, and I felt as close to heaven as I could possibly get while still in the physical body. Their young voices created pure bliss in my soul. I felt warmth radiate into my right foot, feeling the presence of a spirit comforting me. Joy took me into my dreams that night as I remembered.

I never understood what I sensed when I was at the Casa. It was as if I had entered a room covered in beautiful, light-colored, soft fabric. Even my feet felt cushioned. In my mind's eye, I saw a thin, transparent veil in the center of the room. The things that had form were quite solid on the side where I was standing. Those same forms also existed on the other side of the veil, except they were molecules of moving energy. My experiences at the Casa made me wonder about what was real and what was not. The more love I felt, the more radiance came from within me, causing me to reconnect with the feeling of home I had lost at the hour of my mother's death.

This spiritual immersion was the healing of my emotional body. I had found the same home my mother had created through her spirituality—not her religion, but the spirituality that exuded from her being. I understand now why I cried for three weeks after my spiritual surgery at the Casa.

It is now six months later, and the emotional and psychological pain I once knew is gone, completely healed. I never knew this level of healing was possible. I spent a lifetime in therapy and self-help workshops, all of which were great for personal growth but not real healing. Nothing has ever come close to what happened to me when I went before Medium João and the Entities.

▲

MY SON WALKS
"Junior" da Silva

Neusa and Gelson da Silva initially brought their son Junior to the Casa in 1989. He had contracted polio at the age of three months.

Neusa tells her story:
My son was rushed to the hospital with a forty-degree fever (Celsius) after receiving a polio vaccine. Over the next six years, my

husband and I searched desperately for answers, going to doctors and healers, grasping for a cure so he would be able to walk. He had a brace that wrapped around his leg and body right up to his solar plexus. Walking was out of the question. He faced life in a wheelchair.

I first brought Junior to the Casa when he was six years old. The Entity said the treatment would take time, but he would be able to help him. The treatment required that we bring Junior to the Casa every forty days. It was a grueling bus trip. I would bring his books along so he could continue his studies. After one year, his mobility had improved 100 percent, and the Entity took off the brace that covered Junior's right leg and whole torso. The Entity told us that if we had not brought him for treatment when we did, he would have been in a wheelchair permanently. The medical team that had been treating him affirmed this.

Junior continued his treatment with the Entities until his sixteenth year. I honored my commitment to help my son by becoming a Casa guide and helping others. Every forty days, I hired a bus to bring people from my community to the Casa for healing. The bus was always full. The return journey always took longer because we had to make frequent stops to help those who had undergone spiritual surgery and were often throwing up.

The Entity told me in 1999 that we should move to Abadiânia. We had no idea how we would make a living with two sons in school. I asked the Entity to help us. The owners of the Hotel Vila Verde, Ernesto and Izaura, were selling their hotel and were anxious for us to buy it. We did not have the funds to buy the hotel, so they finally agreed they would rent it to us while they searched for a buyer. We moved our whole family. Gelson had to leave his partnership in commercial real estate, and I sold a lucrative business in retail women's clothes. We began our life over again and learned to be hoteliers. It is still a financial struggle. Slowly we learned and began to love our new life.

In 2002, Ernesto and Izaura would not renew our contract and gave us a month's notice because they were going to close the hotel. I returned to Porte Alegre in the south of Brazil to find work and get our sons back into the school system. Gelson was desperate and went to Heather, who always brought her groups to our hotel. Heather and two friends found a way to buy the hotel and leased it to us, so we were able to resume our life in this sanctuary.

Our son walks without crutches now and only has to use a small leg brace. Because our finances are tight, we had to withdraw him from law school at the age of twenty-four, but he is a natural athlete and was playing competitive wheelchair basketball. In 2005, he took up wheelchair tennis and flourished. Thanks to Heather and the sponsorship of her friends and the St. Ignatius Fund, he was able to train with a Dutch coach in São Paulo and travel to Chile to compete internationally. Because of his talent, he was scouted by the Association of Handicapped Sports, founded by Steve Dubener, an American, and is now being trained and receiving a scholarship from them to finish his law degree in São Paulo. I could fill a book with stories of miraculous healings from my twenty years at the Casa. We love Abadiânia. We have found our true home and family here.

▲

GATEWAY TO THE DIVINE
Rosa Haritos

In January 2004, I was hitting my professional stride as an academic researcher at a major Ivy League university. I worked with the top people in my field. Personally, I was on less solid ground: my eleven-year marriage was in disrepair. Waves of anger, fear, and helplessness would wash over me as I watched my husband gradually shut down. After three years of trying conventional therapy, I came to the difficult decision of seeking a divorce. And yet there was a deeper pain, a more profound disconnect from almost everything in my life, a feeling of "is this all there is?" My journey to John of God was twofold: to heal the emotional trauma of my divorce and reconnect spiritually to life.

I arrived at 7:30 A.M. on a Wednesday morning. The Casa was teeming with people of all ages, colors, and ailments. There were wheelchairs, crutches, small children, elderly persons, and at least five different languages being spoken in addition to Brazilian Portuguese broadcast over the loudspeakers. People were queuing up, anxious to be seen by John of God. I stood in silence, small beads of sweat trickling down the back of my neck, eyes closed, trying to take it all in.

I felt a hand brush against me. When I opened my eyes I found a young man deep in meditation, tightly clasping my hand in his. Almost immediately, I felt an electric shock surge through my entire body. I heard a voice speak the exact words that were echoing in my mind: "What was that?" I opened my eyes, expecting to see someone on the other side of me, yet there was no one. The man who held my hand was still deep in prayer. Confused, I turned my gaze across the crowded room and was drawn to a young woman. It was as if we had literally heard each other's thoughts above all the noise, but that seemed impossible. We made our way toward one another, held hands, closed our eyes, and focused on the presence of something greater than us, something divine.

The remainder of my trip was filled with more strange experiences. I could not explain it—given my rigorous scientific training. I saw Technicolor visions with my eyes closed and felt energetic hands as I sat in the current room, gently bending my body, filling it with light and heat. These experiences were not confined to the Casa grounds. On the fourth night of my two-week stay, I felt a presence in my room as I lay in bed. It felt as if two hands gripped my ankles and pressed down hard. I could feel searing heat and pressure rise up into my body, and when it reached my knees, millions of charged needles fired. The pain was overwhelming, but with that thought it lessened. Yet with each breath the hands continued to move up my body, pushing me against the bed. As I looked down at my chest, I could see my body rise up with each movement. I saw bursts of bright light and felt as if someone was realigning my entire spine. Then I felt a hand inside of my mouth, pressing up as waves of electricity pulsed through my teeth, gums, and jaw. Finally, there was a rush of air and the presence was gone. The next morning, I conveyed my story to Heather, who assured me that it was quite common for the Entities to come to our rooms and work on us. I was told not to worry but to trust the process.

I thought about my life as I stood in line that morning. The daughter of immigrant parents, I grew up in a home that was filled with pain and fearfulness. Yet my own direct experiences were so different—I found life to be filled with joy and love, and I embraced it fully. I had passion and a desire to alleviate the world of all suffering. But when my thoughts turned to my marriage, a sorrow weighed upon my heart and soul. I felt lost and ineffective, unable to bridge the chasm that had ripped me away from my husband. Beneath that sorrow was anger, an emotion I preferred to ignore. As these emotions swept over me, I remember asking for help in releasing them, without knowing what that meant or if it were possible.

Heather had instructed me to write my husband's name on a slip of paper, along with his date of birth. I had not brought a photograph, but when I approached the Entity he gently took the piece of paper from my hand and held it. He looked into my eyes with love and compassion, saying, "He is a good man." Once again, I felt as if someone was reading my thoughts, and I smiled. The Entity repeated, "He is a good man," to which I replied, "I know Father, but I can no longer live with him." He took my right hand and began speaking very quickly in Portuguese. Heather said,

"You do not have to do what he is about to tell you." I told Heather I was grateful for the healing I already received and would do anything to relieve the pain in my heart. Again, the Entity said, "You do not have to do what I tell you." I remember feeling confused and impatient, but then Heather explained, "This is about free will. The Entity will offer you advice, but you are free to ignore it."

I looked straight into the Entity's eyes and said, "Father, please tell me." Heather translated, "Get three photos of yourself and be here tomorrow morning on the 8:00 A.M. line. If you do this, I shall give you much happiness in your home." Tears of gratitude streamed down my face as I was ushered into a cab by Heather, who explained to the driver what needed to be done. I was driven to Anápolis and eventually found a passport photo shop in a small mall. I returned to my hotel room that evening, photos in hand, tired and unsure of what awaited me the next morning.

At 8:00 A.M., I was standing in line to see the Entity, clutching my photographs and filled with hope. I approached the Entity, and he took the photographs from me. "Are these your photographs?" he asked.

"Yes, Father," I replied.

A smile. "Are they recent?"

"Yes, Father."

Another smile. "Are you sure?"

Sensing my growing unease, Heather told the Entity about my trip to Anápolis. Once again, he drew me close and held my right hand. "Now I will give you what I promised." At this point I felt a rush of energy into my right hand and was told, "Your faith is strong and has healed you." I was then quickly ushered off the line and instructed to go and "sit in the current room." It was as simple as that—and as complex as that.

On the last day of that trip, while standing in line to say farewell to the Entity, I was told I was a Daughter of the Casa, a member of the Casa family of mediums, and I was given a prescription for herbs. Throughout my two-week stay at the Casa, I had received no surgeries or herbs, just instructions to sit in the current rooms. I was unsure what being a medium entailed, and quite frankly, the very word conjured images of crystal balls and séances. And yet, from what I could surmise, the Casa mediums were faithful, thoughtful men and women who opened themselves to the Divine just by sitting quietly, offering prayers, or directing their consciousness for the benefit of all who traveled to the Casa. My own knowledge about health was based on the premise of alleviating suffering. The *medium* I felt most comfortable with was education and concrete action. Perhaps it was time to look at the bigger picture. I was told to take the herbs and follow three rules: no pork, no alcohol, and no spicy foods or peppers. "Just go about your life as usual," Heather said. Quite frankly, this made little sense, because life as I had known it no longer existed.

Things seemed very different when I got home. Actually, I was different. I tried my best to convey what had happened to me at the Casa, but it was difficult because I was not sure what happened. My anger, fear, and sorrow had been replaced with a spacious openness. I felt humbled by the simplicity of the Casa, the easy and loving environment. I now felt ready to take an honest look at the way in which I conducted my life, with an eye toward releasing what no longer suited me. I found myself drawn into a world I was unfamiliar with: visions throughout the day; sensing energies and hearing thoughts and ideas that were not my own; and that familiar energetic hand on my back. As these experiences grew stronger, I realized I needed help to navigate this new world. I immersed myself in shamanic training for the next two years, spending countless hours learning about the gift of mediumship and the responsibility that comes with serving others.

I return to the Casa every year and expect to continue this pilgrimage, not only out of gratitude but also a desire to serve the other people who make their way to see this amazing healer. My husband visited the Casa for a week in the summer of 2005, and he has also experienced a reconnection with what he holds Divine. We have been working hard at our marriage and have made some remarkable progress—something neither of us thought possible. There is still much to be done, but we are willing to do it together, with the love and support of the Casa Entities.

There is a saying that tells us to study the finger that points to the moon. For me, the Casa is that finger—a beacon of light that called me home, warmed my soul, and provided a safe container for me to reconnect to my own light and awaken from my deep sleep of indifference. I learned that as long as I live and act from my heart, right action follows.

▲

A SECOND CHANCE
John Friesman

John had grown to disdain the time of day when his body was compelled to purge itself over and over. He lived with a constant, violent headache. There was no relief, and over the course of months John had visited his doctor numerous times. With depression as the diagnosis and Prozac as the cure, John finally found a doctor who sent him to Auckland Hospital for an MRI.

John tells his story:
I received the shock of my life in July 1998. The doctor who gave me the MRI asked me to wait in the corridor while he had a quick look at the scan. When he came to deliver the results, I noted he had become pale. He explained that in his seventeen years of working in medicine he had never seen a brain tumor as large as mine.

He immediately put me into surgery to relieve the pressure in my brain. During the surgery, he inserted a shunt valve into my stomach, with a tube that went from my belly to my brain and another valve in my skull. I felt fantastic after this, but the doctors warned me it was only the beginning. They needed to "de-bulk" the tumor because of its size. A second, more dangerous procedure was done two days later. This was a ten-and-a-half-hour operation, and they lost me twice, resuscitating me each time and then closing me up with only half the tumor removed because it was too dangerous to continue. The egg-sized tumor had also grown into my first vertebra so they removed a third of the vertebra trying to get any roots. They gave me massive doses of radiation after sewing me up plus large amounts of steroids.

They discharged me and told me to go home, even though I was extremely weak and violently ill. I had massive stomach pains on the way home and stopped when I saw my ex-partner's car. She said I looked terrible and shouldn't be left by myself. I wouldn't be able to survive. She took me to her house, gave me her bed, and nursed me for seven weeks. I had sixty-six peptic ulcers. I stopped eating and drinking at one point. I would never have gotten through it without an old woman, Mrs. Rebecca Parks, who visited me. She said she couldn't stand the way I looked. She went home and made up a jug of barley water. She brought it to me, warmed it up, and even though others had given me up for dead, she stayed with me every day until the entire jug was gone. She drip-fed the water down my throat. After that, I actually recovered.

I was in remission for one year. During that time, I went to Auckland Hospital every three months. "All clear," they'd tell me. "Go home." I was very happy with myself, until on one such check the doctor just looked at the ground. He read gruesome statistics. "Fifty percent of the people with your type of tumor are dead within five years, but you don't have anywhere near that much time." He told me the tumor was growing rapidly right through my brain. It had become inoperable and there was nothing the doctors could do for me. I couldn't stand to hear anymore of it and ran out of the hospital crying. The doctor came after me, saying, "Johnny, listen, we can give you morphine when you become bedridden." That was the last thing I needed to hear.

I went to a phone and called my Dad. I said, "Dad, I'm dying." My Dad is a Dutchman, a hard, stubborn man. He said, "Look, boy, don't give up. We will ring up every hospital in the world, if necessary, until we find someone who can help you." But they all had the same answer. There really was nothing they could do for me. At one hospital in Melbourne, Australia, they said that they could use me as a guinea pig to try some experimental drugs but that I'd most likely be dead within twelve months.

I had nowhere to turn. Then I received a phone call from an older man, Mr. Howard, from Great Barrier. When I was a child and butchering, I use to bring meat to his family when they would come over to the island on holiday. I had not really seen much of him since then. He said that he had a dream the night before. "I was told I was to show you something." He was with his daughter in Auckland, and he asked me to come up and see what it was. I was baffled by this, but I had nothing to lose so I flew to Auckland. He showed me a video of John of God. I was determined to see this healer. There was only one phone number on the tape. It was of a young man who had crushed a vertebra in an accident and went to John of God for help. I called him. He told me he could only stand for about one hour when he first came to the Casa a few years before. He had been fully cured. He was going out windsurfing that day and felt fantastic.

It gave me faith. He gave me the phone number for Bernadette Andrews, who takes people to John of God from New Zealand. At first, she would not take me without a release from my doctors, but they would not give me one. Bernadette kindly asked the Entities whether I should go. They told her to use her own discretion, so she took me on her next trip.

There were seventeen of us who went in front of the Entities that first day. I was in so much pain that I was walking on my tiptoes.

I could not stop crying from the pain. John of God came out on the little stage in front of us. There were hundreds around us, but he seemed to look straight at me, walking toward me. I was elated. I thought I would be cured, but at the last second he veered to his right and went over to a Brazilian man. There was a woman holding an instrument tray. He took a scalpel and started scraping this man's eyeballs. I watched intently with every stroke. The man was in no pain; he never flinched. I do a lot of chainsaw work and know what sawdust in the eye can feel like. Yet, here was this man not even moving. I was upset that Medium João had not worked on me. But, later on, the Entities scheduled me for surgery the following morning.

The next day, I went into the surgery room and waited for John of God. When he came in, he first said the Lord's Prayer. I had my eyes closed and my right hand on the back of my head. The nonphysical surgery had begun. My neck and head seemed to become a bit softer under my hand, and I felt like butterflies were fluttering underneath my skin. It was amazing. Before I knew it, one of the aides said I could go home now because my operation was complete. I walked outside and suddenly realized I was walking on my feet with no pain. I was told to go back to my hotel and rest for twenty-four hours.

As I got out of the taxi, I was so elated to be without pain that I jumped up and down to see if it was real—just what I had been asked not to do. Bernadette explained sternly that this was a "true surgery" with possible internal stitches. Would you be jumping around after brain surgery in a hospital?

I was to go before the Entity again after seven days to have my review. I wrote a note thanking John of God and the Entities for a second chance at life. I was told to return when I felt ready. I gained strength and had no headaches or vomiting for a year. But then, in July 2000, I began to have headaches again. I returned to the Casa for a second surgery and was told afterward that I was fully cured.

I returned home and have been pain-free ever since. I had an MRI a few years ago to verify the healing. My physician, Dr. McDonald, was baffled by the results. The egg-shaped mass had been reduced to a small dormant nub at the base of my skull. The doctor decided I needed no other treatment.

I tell my story to anyone who wishes to hear. I show videos to repay John of God for my new life, and if asked, I am willing to help anyone visit this amazing healer.

▲

THE CLOCK WAS TICKING
Barbara Ettleson

On March 27, 2002, I was diagnosed with breast cancer, an all too common diagnosis for women in this country. My doctor wanted me to have a double mastectomy; after all, I had fibrocystic breasts, and it was difficult to get a clear mammogram reading. I was in shock. My surgeon told me he'd expect a decision in three days; this was a Thursday. On Friday, I went with my partner and a friend to visit the radiologist and oncologist. The oncologist told me that nothing but surgery and radiation and chemotherapy would work. "Don't even think about herbs," he said. "This is cancer." The radiologist was the most helpful and explained the radiation protocol. The Methodist Hospital in Des Moines, Iowa, didn't use Sentinel Node Biopsy as their standard of care, which meant that all my lymph nodes were under scrutiny. I was scared and fast becoming depressed. The clock was ticking.

I awoke Saturday morning remembering about a spiritual teacher's trip to John of God in Brazil. I called the teacher, and she encouraged me to go. She gave me the name of a person who took people to see John of God. My teacher told me that this woman had just returned from Brazil and might not be heading back there soon but to call her anyway. My teacher told me I might have to wait for a call back but to not be discouraged. I hung up with my teacher and called Heather Cumming. She answered and told me she was headed back to Brazil in two weeks on personal business but would be glad to take us to see John of God. Within two weeks, we managed to get our passports and sell a house and buy a new one, and now we were headed to Brazil.

Once on the flight to Brazil, the world slowed down. Our pilgrimage had begun. It took us thirty hours to arrive in the town where John of God performs his miraculous healing. Heather met us in Brasília and took us under her care. We had several days to prepare ourselves before seeing John of God. This was a very healing and loving journey. We spent time in a small church in old Abadiânia, reputed to have been visited by Mary, praying and talking and being held in great love by the spirits of the church. We meditated at the waterfall on the Casa property. We were greeted by many Divas and, most incredibly, a snake met us on the path when we were coming up from the waterfall, a clear sign of transformation.

John of God told me to prepare for surgery and sent me to spend time meditating on the healing I needed. The staff at the Casa encouraged me to focus on love and forgiveness while I meditated. The kindness of the Casa personnel helped me stay centered, hopeful, and filled with a sense of calm and love as I approached the work I was to do. John of God told me to return three times and gave me herbs to take in between my trips to see him. We returned three times, and on the last visit he declared me healed. I was honored to be asked to speak to others who had come to John of God for healing.

In addition to our spiritual work in Brazil, my partner and I changed our diet. We worked with the Kushi Institute in Beckett, Mass., and followed a strict regimen. We were then enrolled in a three-year program of shamanic work through the Foundation for Shamanic Studies. Under the instruction of Sandra

Ingerman we received much healing through working with her and our fellow healers.

After my return from my third trip to Brazil, I decided to have a thermograph reading to ascertain the health of my breasts. I had a series of readings over a six-month period. At the end of the six months, my doctor explained that the breast-heat readings were so consistently slow that I "must have been misdiagnosed."

I will never know whether or not I was misdiagnosed. What I do know is that love, forgiveness, a devoted and loving partner, healthy eating, and the support and wisdom of the spirits is what worked for me. Everyone walks their own path, and mine is not right for every one. But I believe that cancer was a gift given to me and that I brought it about. And since I had brought it about, only I could release it. I am grateful for my experiences and try every day to appreciate the gift of healing from the spirits and those who accompanied me on the journey.

▲

AFTER THREE DECADES OF DEAFNESS
Barbara Brodsky

I made my first trip to the Casa in January 2004 with the hope they could heal my deafness. I lost my hearing in 1972, just after my first child was born. During childbirth, the nerves were oxygen-starved and died, leaving me deaf and without balance. Doctors in the United States said there was no cure. For decades I lived with the situation, learning to lip-read and relying on a walking stick for balance. Then someone sent me material about the Casa, and I decided to go.

The first step was to look at the possibility of hearing. It seems wonderful, but I had to be honest with myself. Deafness was also an escape from unpleasantness. If someone was angry, I could avert my gaze. When the world news was unpleasant, I could stop reading the captions. If my children were noisy, I just looked away. After three decades of deafness, I was used to living in some degree of seclusion. I saw the deafness in many ways as a gift, one that had led me to my life's work as a meditation teacher. What would it mean to hear? What would I lose?

The months before the first visit were intense, as I looked at the intention to hear and what hearing meant in a deeper way. By the time my flight took off, I felt ready. The Entities told me they probably could help me. It would take time and I would need to return, but that was fine.

Three months after my first visit, I was in a terrible accident in which I was tossed against the ocean floor by a large wave. I was pulled unconscious from the ocean, near death. Many of my bones were broken, including facial bones, and my vision was severely diminished. Now I wasn't only deaf but blind in one eye, with poor vision in the other, and in severe pain. Yet in those moments in the ocean I had made a decision for life. And the body would heal; my neck and back were not broken, which I knew was a gift from the Entities. I had felt them with me in that moment of impact. I focused on healing the broken bones and exploring what it meant to choose life and fully embrace it. I could feel the energy and support of the entities in my meditation.

My next trip to Brazil was in February 2005. Again, I asked for healing of my deafness and also my vision. I went with 20/200 vision in one eye and 20/100 vision in the other. I returned home a month later with the better eye 20/20, the other 20/50, and immense gratitude for the world that had been returned to me. Choosing life! That healing led me back to the question, what does it mean to heal? It's not only the body that heals, but the healing is about karma and my entire relationship with the world. To hear and see fully is to be completely intimate with the world. Yet, we all protect ourselves, armor ourselves in some ways. As a meditation teacher, I find that for many people, separation is the greatest pain. We separate from the world, from those around us, and from ourselves.

The year 2005 brought its own challenges, because medical treatment in the United States again diminished my vision. When I returned to the Casa in January 2006, one eye was totally blind, and now, two years after my first trip, there was still no change at all in my hearing. In 2005, the Entity had asked me to buy a complete set of tuning forks and sound them near each ear daily in order to "hear" the sound waves and sing the tones. I was an expert at this now and was able to recognize the vibrations and sing in tune. But I still couldn't hear normal speech or even a firecracker. As the trip approached, there were doubts. Am I deluding myself? Should I give up?

Early in my 2006 visit, one of the Entities asked me with such compassionate eyes and expression, "Why do you wish to see and hear?" It brought me full circle to that early reflection about allowing full intimacy with the world. I knew it wasn't asked as a challenge so much as a suggestion that I develop more inner clarity. My first thought was a wish to hear the beauty of a child's laughter, the sweet music of a stream flowing over rocks, the sigh of the breeze in the trees, music; to see the beauty of the rainbow, a smile, the dewdrops. But immediately I knew that wasn't enough. Along with all those sounds and sights are the harsh and difficult ones: the terrible screams of beings in agony, the roar of a tidal wave or erupting volcano, the cries of grief, the violence of a bomb dropped, limbs torn off and flying through the air.

At first, I said, "I'm willing to see and hear it all." Then I realized an amendment was needed. I want to see and hear it all. Only through intimacy with what some call the ten thousand joys and sorrows does the heart truly open. It's only here that we begin to know true compassion. Can I then say that I want to hear and see to better know compassion? I spent several days with that question. The end isn't compassion but unconditional love. Only love allows us to be fully present to ourselves and others; only love can bring forth change. Compassion is the path, and intimacy and presence are the companions to compassion.

Is there a voyeuristic component to hearing and seeing so as to experience? I acknowledge that's part of it: a little greed, wanting to gain something, to be filled. But that part isn't willing to be intimate with the pain, only to survey it from outside. The motivation must go deeper, into that place which aspires to know unconditional love and to serve from that place of love.

The Entity's question drew me to see the destination more clearly, the aspiration to service and to love, and the intention to open ever more fully to everything. Then I had to ask myself, do I need physical vision and hearing to reach this goal? No. Then why do I want to hear and see? Here my heart finally opened deeply to the immense sadness of what had been lost, the sense of limitation I'd developed from my lost hearing and limited vision.

I experience equanimity now, at some level. But I also see how I had withdrawn through the years, with a subtle "sour grapes" attitude. There was failure to trust the true possibilities of connection, to trust the capacity of the heart to love, and to hold pain with love. Deafness was just the scapegoat. Then what needs to be healed? Not the eyes. Not the ears. But the separation. I open to the "ever-healed," to that which knows its divinity, wholeness, and innate perfection.

As I reflected on this, the question returned, why do I want to hear and see? For joy! It's not just that ego wants experience. Love invites joyful experience just for the wonder of it. That intention needed to be honored, love's intention to ever more deeply know itself. I saw the part of me that felt some grasping and could offer it kindness, and also the part that felt some shame at asking for hearing, thinking of it only as physical sensation. Both still arise in the human. Let them be and turn to that which seeks in joy and love.

I finally understand that this was the deeper healing, which the Entities understood the need for long before I did. They didn't create the wave accident, of course. Our lives draw us where we need to be, and one experience or a parallel one will come. But they helped me to use that experience to stop armoring myself in any way, to open my heart to the world and to myself. In their wisdom they didn't just "fix" the outer symptom, which I know they could have done, but asked me to heal the inner wounds.

This was a needed first step. My eye improves, and I know my hearing will, too. This year, they smiled at my tuning fork demonstration and said the work was right on track. They are working on my ears. Interestingly, while I do choose to hear, I no longer need to hear, because I hear it all now through my other senses. The barriers are gone. I am complete, and hearing will be a wonderful extra gift!

Heather comments:
On March 14, 2006, the week after Barbara returned home to America, Dr. Valdivino announced in a loud voice for the current to hear, "Your friend, the woman who is deaf, I am helping her. Tell her I am taking care of her."

To learn more about these and other remarkable healing stories, visit *www.healingquests.com.*

AFTERWORD

Our book, gradually conceived through the guidance and blessings of the Entities, began as a book of testimonials. It was quite evident as we began writing, often awakening at 4:00 A.M., inspired by the Spirits, that the text was also to become a guidebook for travelers to the Casa and a brief look into the life of the man, John of God. It is often said that the veils between the spiritual realms and the earth are very thin in Abadiânia. As a result, the spirits are able to touch our lives in very profound and tangible ways. Those who return from their pilgrimage often captivate us with stories of extraordinary miracles they've witnessed or heard about. It is our sincere hope that this book removes some of the mystery of this process. It is our experience that those who travel to the Casa heed a call and act on it; they solemnly engage in a commitment to evaluate their lives and reconnect with what they hold Divine. It can be a daunting endeavor, and sometimes the rewards are slow in coming or are not quite what we expected. So why would one choose to pilgrimage to the Casa and what causes one to return again?

The Entities tells us that we belong to a single spiritual family. The Entities love us all, equally and unconditionally. At the Casa de Dom Inácio de Loyola, pilgrims come together with the intention of being seen, heard, and healed. They bear witness to this process not only in themselves but in others as well. It is this convergence of energy—this palpable willingness to participate in the healing of the collective—that reaches the spiritual realms of the loving and compassionate Entities. They, too, heed the call and make their presence known as they oversee our individual healing and the healing of our planet.

We thank Medium João and Ana for allowing us into their lives and speaking candidly with us. To the Casa staff, volunteers, and all of those who shared their stories with us, we thank you. And to the loving and compassionate Entities of light, we are most grateful for your love and support of our project.

We leave you with the words of Medium João: "God is the Architect of the universe, the supreme intelligence. God is in everything all of the time. My message to you is to practice charity and fraternal love. All are welcome here."

We are all blessed by the words of the Entities resounding out into the world: "*Fica na paz de Deus*—Stay with the peace of God."

If you are inspired by this book to go to Abadiânia, there is no greater gift you can give yourself than a pilgrimage to this sacred land. A two-week trip, particularly for the first visit, is greatly enhanced by going with a guided group. Bearing witness to the healing process of others and actively participating in this dynamic will dissolve differences and barriers so that in the end, it is not "your" or "my" healing but "our" healing that allows us to reconnect with that which is meaningful in our lives.

Go to *www.friendsofthecasa.org* for detailed information about hotels in Abadiânia and official tour guides to the Casa. For information regarding tours to visit John of God with Heather Cumming and updated testimonials, go to *www.healingquests.com* or *www.johnofgodtours.com.* For updated information, including the opportunity to view and purchase spirit photos, current-room photos of the Entities, video interviews, and other blessed products from the Casa de Dom Inácio de Loyola, go to *www.beyondword.com.* For additional photos taken by Karen Leffler or to take photographic journeys to sacred sites with Karen, visit *www.worthathousandwords.info* and *www.spiritfotos.com.*

ACKNOWLEDGMENTS

We are honored and grateful for the encouragement of the Entities who coaxed and inspired us. We thank John of God for incorporating these spirits for the selfless purpose of healing others—and for telling us he had "complete faith and trust" in our ability to write this book. We also acknowledge the Divine Spirit that dwells in each human being.

To our friends and companions who shared their stories with us, thank you. "Shungo"—from our hearts to your hearts. A special thanks to Jenny Lauren, Janice Papolos, and Judy Ostrow for their encouragement in finding a publisher. To Richard Cohn and Cindy Black for sharing our vision; and editors Jessica Bryan, Henry Covi, and Rosa Haritos—our gratitude is beyond words. We also thank those who shared our tears of joy and tears of fear: JoAnn Wolff, Barbara Conetta, Veronica Willson, Maureen Adler, Pam Garner, Trudy Griswold, Linda Hooper, Denise Gross, Susan Grunebaum, Jane Brown, Nancy Cingari, Lucy Walker, Eileen Karn, Martin and Fernanda, Bill Walker, Maninho and Lucia,

Gelson and Neusa, Nancy and Kathy, Donna Whittaker, Mignon Lawless, and Anthony Smokovich.

To Cokie Lewis, Pat, Barbara, and Sandra Ingerman, teacher and mentor; to Sebastian, our gentle guide; and to all the others who have touched our hearts, thank you. Karen acknowledges Heather's children for the deep joy they have brought her. Heather gives special thanks to her children, Sasha and Ben—your love, support, and encouragement mean the world to me. Thank you for choosing me as your "mumma" and accepting me unconditionally with all my quirks and idiosyncrasies. You are my teachers. Te amo pra la de todas as luas! Dan, obrigado Senhor!

BIBLIOGRAPHY
AND SUGGESTED READING

BIBLIOGRAPHY

Bragdon, Emma. *Kardec's Spiritism: A Home for Healing and Spiritual Evolution.* Woodstock, Vt.: Lightening Up Press, 2000.

Brodsky, Barbara. *Presence, Kindness and Freedom.* Ann Arbor, Mich.: Deep Spring Press, 2003.

Butler, Alban. *Lives of the Saints.* Collegeville, Minn.: Liturgical Press, 2003.

Carman, Philip. *Ignatius Loyola.* New York: Harper & Row, 1990.

Coleridge, Henry James. *Life and Letters of St. Francis Xavier.* London: Burnes and Oates, 1876.

Emoto, Masaru. *The Secret Life of Water.* New York: Beyond Words Publishing/Atria Books, 2005.

Garcia, Ismar Estulano. *Curas Espirituais.* Goiânia, Brazil: AB Editora, 2006.

Goswami, Amit. *Physics of the Soul.* Charlottesville, Va.: Hampton Roads Publishing, 2001.

————. *The Quantum Doctor: A Physicist's Guide to Health and Healing.* Charlottesville, Va.: Hampton Roads Publishing, 2004.

————. *The Self-Aware Universe: How Consciousness Creates the Material World.* New York: Putnam's Sons, 1993.

Ignatius of Loyola, Saint. *The Spiritual Exercises of Saint Ignatius.* New York: P. J. Kenedy, 1963.

Ingerman, Sandra. *Medicine for the Earth: How to Transform Personal and Environmental Toxins.* New York: Three Rivers Press, 1994.

Kardec, Allan. *The Book on Mediums.* New York: Samuel Weiser, 1970.

————. *Genesis.* New York: The Spiritist Alliance for Books, 2003.

————. *The Gospel Explained by the Spiritist Doctrine.* Philadelphia: Allan Kardec Educational Society, 2000.

————. *Heaven and Hell.* New York: The Spiritist Alliance for Books, 2003.

————. *Le Livre des Esprits.* Paris, France: Elibron Classics Edition, 1861.

————. *The Spirits' Book: Inspiration and Resolution for the Questioning Soul.* Philadelphia: Allan Kardec Educational Society, 2003.

Kardec, Allan, and Emma A. Wood. *Experimental Spiritism: Book on Mediums, or a Guide for Mediums and Invocators.* Whitefish, Mont.: Kessinger Publishing, 1874.

Korngold, Jussara, and Marie Levinson, transl. *Endearing Gems from Francisco Cândido Xavier.* New York: Spiritist Alliance for Books, 2005.

MacKenzie, Kenneth R. H. *The Royal Masonic Cyclopaedia of History, Rites, Symbolism, and Biography.* New York: J. W. Bouton, 1877.

McGregor, Pedro. *Jesus of the Spirits.* New York: Stein and Day, 1967.

O'Malley, John W. *The First Jesuits.* Cambridge: Harvard University Press, 1993.

Pellegrino-Estrich, Robert. *The Miracle Man: The Life Story of João de Deus.* Goiânia, Goiás, Brazil: Grapica Terra, 2002.

Povoa, Liberaro. *João de Deus Fenomeno de Abadiânia*. Anápolis, Goiás, Brazil: Múltipla Gráfica e Editora Ltda., 1994.

Roberston, Elizabeth, and Elias Amidor. *Life Prayers from Around the World*. New York: HarperCollins, 1996.

Savaris, Alfredina Arlete. *"Curas Paranormais Realizadas por João Teixeira de Faria."* 1977 post-graduate thesis, University of Dr. Bezerra de Menezes, Curitiba, Brazil.

Sicardo, Joseph. *St. Rita of Cascia: Saint of the Impossible*. Rockford, Ill.: TAN Books, 2003.

Xavier, Francisco Cândido, [psychographed from Andre Luiz]. *And Life Goes On...* Philadelphia: Allan Kardec Educational Society, 2000.

————. *Nosso Lar: A Spiritual Home*. Philadelphia: Allan Kardec Educational Society, 2000.

SUGGESTED READING

Hicks, Esther. *The Amazing Power of Deliberate Intent*. Carlsbad, Calif.: Hay House, 2005.

Spalding, Baird T. *Life and Teaching of the Masters of the Far East*. Marina del Rey, Calif.: DeVorss Publications, 1927.

RavenWing, Josie. *The Book of Miracles: The Healing Work of João de Deus*. Bloomington, Ind.: AuthorHouse, 2005.

WEB RESOURCES

For more information on the Oswaldo Cruz Foundation, please visit the Portuguese website http://www.fiocruz.br.

For more information about Spiritism, please visit the Spiritist Group of New York website http://www.sgny.org.

For more information on the history of Brazil, please visit http://www.infobrasilia.com.br/bsb_h5i.htm.

For more information on Bezerra de Menezes, please visit the Portuguese website http://www.franciscodeassis.org.br/bio.php.

For an article on the history of the Oswaldo Cruz Foundation
written by its president, Paulo Buss (*The Oswaldo Cruz Foundation:
100 Years*, TDR News 65, 2001), please visit http://www.who
.int/tdr/publications/tdrnwes/news65/oswaldo-ruz.htm.

For more information on Francisco Cândido (Chico) Xavier, please
visit the Portuguese website http://www.chicoxavieruberaba
.com.br/biografia.htm.

To order Ismar Estulano Garcia's book *Curas Espirituais*, please visit the
Portuguese website AB Editora http://www.abeditora.com.br.